CURRENT AFRICAN ISSUES No 66

FROM ASWAN
TO STIEGLER'S GORGE

Small Stories About Large Dams

Edited by
Terje Oestigaard, Atakilte Beyene and Helga Ögmundardóttir

NORDISKA AFRIKAINSITUTET
The Nordic Africa Institute

UPPSALA 2019

INDEXING TERMS:

Dams
Rivers
Water management
Irrigation
Hydroelectric power
Development projects
Politics
Nile River
Egypt
Ethiopia
Sudan
Tanzania
Uganda

From Aswan to Stiegler's Gorge : Small stories about large dams
Current African Issues No 66

Edited by Terje Oestigaard, Atakilte Beyene and Helga Ögmundardóttir

ISSN 0280-2171
ISBN 978-91-7106-833-0   print-on-demand version
ISBN 978-91-7106-834-7   pdf e-book

Layout and production editor: Henrik Alfredsson, the Nordic Africa Institute
Language editor: Clive Liddiard

Front cover: Ribb Dam under construction, Amhara state, Ethiopia, October 2014. Photo credit Beatrice Mosello, ODI.

THE NORDIC AFRICA INSTITUTE (Nordiska Afrikainstitutet) conducts independent, policy-relevant research, provides analysis and informs decision-making, advancing research-based knowledge of contemporary Africa.

The opinions expressed in this volume are those of the author(s) and do not necessarily reflect the views of the Nordic Africa Institute.

This work is freely available in open access, you can download it online via the NAI web site, www.nai.uu.se, where you can also purchase print edition copies.

Contents

Contributors

Terje Oestigaard is an archaeologist, researcher and Docent at the Department of Archaeology and Ancient History, Uppsala University, Sweden. Since 2006, he has worked with the Nile basin countries and conducted fieldworks in Egypt, Ethiopia, Tanzania and Uganda. Previous to his research in Africa, he conducted contemporary and archaeological fieldworks in Bangladesh, Greece, Jordan, India, Nepal, Palestine as well as in Scandinavia. He is also the author of *The Religious Nile. Water, Ritual and Society since Ancient Egypt* (I.B. Tauris, London, 2018).

Atakilte Beyene holds a PhD from the Swedish University of Agricultural Sciences and has worked in universities and research institutes in Sweden and Ethiopia. His research focuses on agrarian and rural institutions, natural resource management, food security and gender studies. He has conducted extensive field studies in Ethiopia and Tanzania. He has both coordinated and worked on interdisciplinary research projects in Nordic and African countries. His current research includes large-scale agricultural and irrigation investments in Africa, and their implications for local economies.

Helga Ögmundardóttir is a lecturer at the Faculty of Sociology, Anthropology and Folkloristics at Háskóli Íslands, the university of Iceland. She holds a PhD in cultural anthropology at the Universtity of Uppsala, Sweden. Her research fields are environmental anthropology, environmental and resource management, qualitative methodology, human ecology, and socio-cultural effects of climate change.

Kjell Havnevik, phd, is professor emeritus at the Department of Global Development and Planning, the University of Agder, Norway. He has more than four decades of experience of research, education and supervision from Norwegian, Swedish and Tanzanian research institutions and universities. His focus is on agriculture and rural development, natural resource management, the role of international financial- and aid institutions, in particular the World Bank, IMF and Nordic ones, in East and Southern Africa.

Ana Elisa Cascão is an independent consultant and researcher working in the field of transboundary water management and cooperation. Previously she worked as a Programme Manager at the Stockholm International Water Institute (2010-2017). Her latest co-authored book is entitled *The Grand Ethiopian Renaissance Dam and the Nile Basin: Implications for Transboundary Water Cooperation* (Routledge, 2017). She is currently working on a Special Issue entitled *Water Security in the Nile Basin: Understanding and expanding the solution space* (forthcoming 2019).

Terje Oestigaard, Atakilte Beyene and Kjell Havnevik have all worked at different period as senior researchers at the Nordic Africa Institute.

Preface and acknowledgements

This volume in the Current African Issues series is based on the workshop 'Dams, Decisions, Discourses and Developments in Nile Basin Countries', held on 2 November 2017 at Reykjavik's Nordic House (Norræna húsið) and National Museum (Þjóðminjasafnið). The workshop was co-organised by the Nordic Africa Institute (Uppsala), Faculty of sociology, anthropology and folkloristics, University of Iceland, and the Directorate for International Development Cooperation/Ministry for Foreign Affairs (Iceland). We would like to thank all participants and partners, and in particular Þórdís Sigurðardóttir, Pétur Skúlason Waldorff and Jón Geir Pétursson. Lastly, Henrik Alfredsson deserves special thanks not only for making the maps and illustrations used in this publication, but also for doing an impressive job with the layout.

Terje Oestigaard, Atakilte Beyene and Helga Ögmundardóttir

The Nordic House in Reykjavik, opened 1968. Architect Alvar Aalto. Photo: Þorsteinn V. Jónsson, Flickr.

The tension between countries over access to Nile water will probably rise, as spells of drought increase in length and intensity.

/ Helga Ögmundardóttir, p. 15

Asswan High Dam in Egypt, April 2009. Photo by Cliff Hellis, Flickr.

8

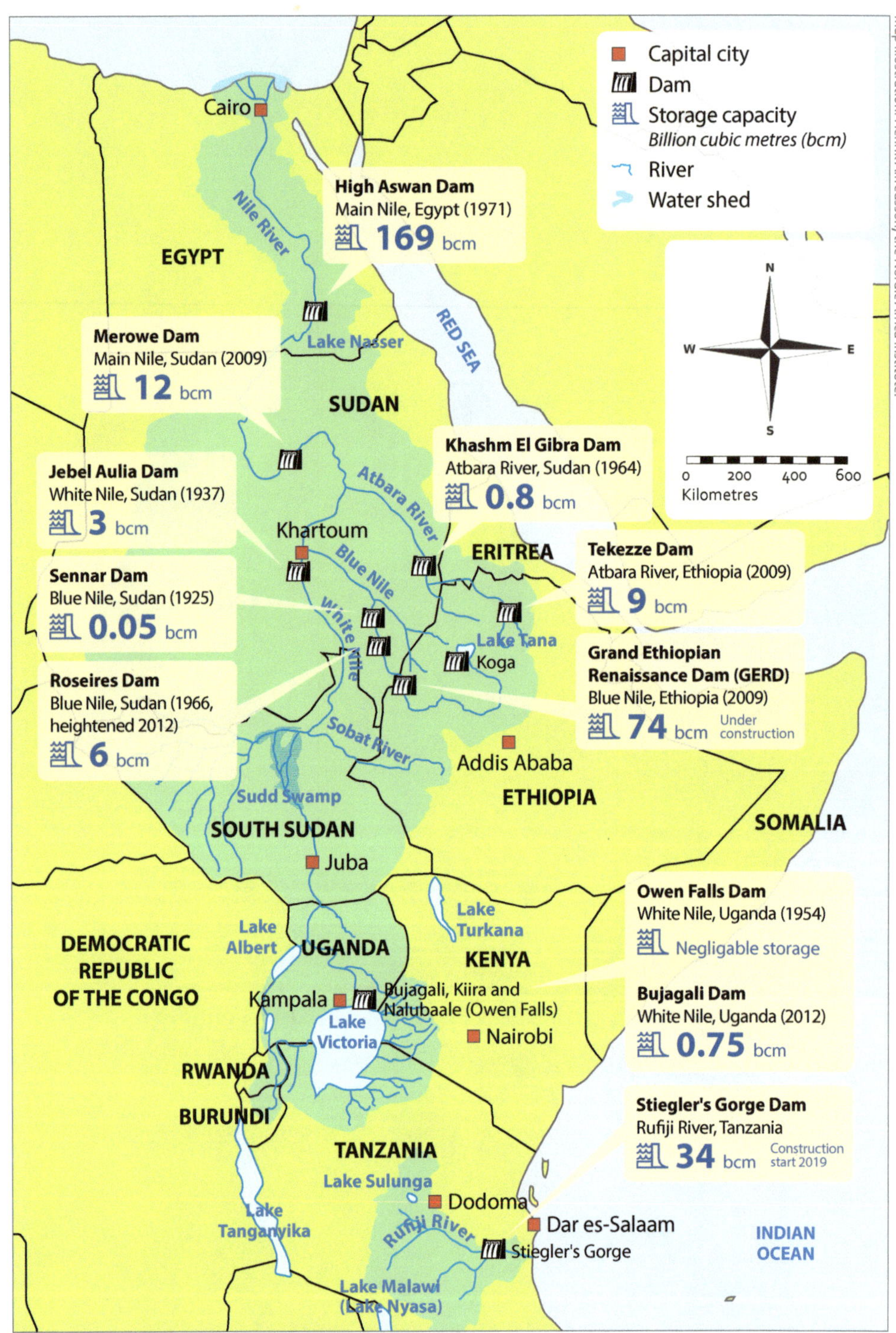

Figure 1.1. The Nile Basin covers approximately 3.25 million square kilometres, about 10 per cent of the area of Africa. The catchment basin for the Rufiji River complex is 177,000 square kilometres. Source for data on year of completion and approximate storage capacity: Cascão, 2019.

CHAPTER 1

What are rivers for? Some theoretical issues of building dams and nations

Helga Ögmundardóttir

Few natural phenomena have inspired the human imagination like rivers, with their different shapes and forms, meanings and landscapes, wonders and dangers. The ways in which people think about them and interpret their characteristics and natures are as varied as the histories of human–river interactions from ancient times to the present. They can see rivers as useful or dangerous, as living beings, life-givers – or wasted megawatts, if not harnessed. Every river has its own cosmology in people's minds, and this is communicated between individuals and groups over generations, and often over vast geographical distances. These riverine cosmologies should be included in their hydrological histories, just as their natural histories are, as well as the more technological implications of how they can be harnessed.

The unique history and cosmology of the Nile is one such central narrative of human–river co-existence, making it a powerful symbol for people all over the world. The local people living in the area that the Nile feeds with essential water have, throughout time, developed management systems and ideologies which form the basis for today's activities focusing on the Nile – damming among them. Few human activities affect a river in such a profound way as a dam, whether intended for hydropower production or water management and irrigation. The planning, building and operating of a dam, with all the associated technological, aesthetic, historical, economic, socio-cultural and political ideologies, discourses and knowledge, form part of a river's cosmology that unfolds over time as they are conceived, created, pondered and – last but not least – disputed. Dams are a central part of development plans and ideologies in many countries (not least developing ones); but they are also at the heart of environmental issues – increasingly so, as unharnessed rivers become ever rarer in the world.

The hydropolitics of dams

This introductory chapter will list some important issues involving the hydropolitics of dams. It is not an exhaustive list, but it should give an idea of how complex and multi-faceted the issue is. Hydropolitics forms a complex web of discourse, but often only a part of what can be said about rivers and their catchments appears in the public space of governance, politics and the media. However, the cultural and ideological aspects are perhaps the most urgent topics to address nowadays, in a world of population growth and increased competition over resources such as arable land and usable water. This is also a world where governments face the growing bargaining power of multinational corporations and emerging superpower states. Besides dealing with the increased globalisation of corporate power, they have to deal with other nation states (often their neighbours) seeking energy, food and resources for their peoples. These politics are played out in and between governments and parliaments, public groupings and organisations, national and international institutions. And they are expressed in environmental impact assessments, contracts, the media and other venues where we get a glimpse of what is unfolding.

Issues surrounding dams in the Nile are like the river itself, its catchment area, and its dependent societies in the riparian states – big, complex and situated in a profound historical and geographical context. Some issues are the same, whereas others are more locally specific; but all are relevant in any general overview of the building of dams and their connected management activities. This applies not least to the differences surrounding each case and concerning both the particular moment in time when they take place and their specific location. Seen from the collective content of this book, it is evident that, in order to understand the issue of dams in the Nile, it is important to locate each case of damming in the wider context of land and resource use, with a focus on models of user rights and ownership, access and the exclusion of different groups from land and water. This includes the official and expressed purpose on the one hand, and on the other hand – and even more importantly – the more hidden processes of finance and politics, which have to be mapped. Crucial questions include what the water, hydropower, revenues, etc. are to be used for; who will benefit and who will lose out from a damming project; and who controls the money borrowed to build such huge structures.

As bodies of water – the stuff of life – rivers cannot but become the subject of symbolism and metaphor, value and wealth, and even ideas of otherworldly existence and power. They are bound to be contested, as different groups see them in different ways, depending on how they see themselves in relation to the rivers. The nearness (or remoteness) of human settlements to rivers, the potential the water has for people, and the size, shape and situation in the landscape of rivers all shape access to water. When researching rivers and dams, one has to be careful to look at the issues not only from an instrumental–functional point of view (engineering, politics, economics, resource extraction and resource management), but also from a cultural, ecological, conservation, epistemological and existential perspective.

To take one of these issues as an example, one can consider the role of national and international environmental NGOs, which often seek support for nature conservation projects in tropical and sub-tropical areas. The protection of rivers like the Amazon and the Nile are good examples of this: many environmental NGOs stress the rivers' existential value and their centrality to the earth's ecosystem. Other NGOs – not least those focusing on development projects in developing countries – are also important players, and the interaction of these non-governmental and often global agents is an important, rather under-investigated topic both within and between various states. The involvement of indigenous peoples and other local groups in damming disputes on many of the earth's biggest rivers is getting increased attention, as are gender issues and the uneven distribution among women and men of both benefits and adverse effects. These sides of damming have to be addressed, particularly if damming projects are to be more sustainable – in every sense of the term: environmental, economic and socio-cultural. This could even, in certain cases, entail certification of social and environmental responsibility, according to the international bodies that provide such services. But it is no less essential to scrutinise both the expected and planned outcomes of a dam and the unanticipated aspects, both positive and negative. Given the huge (direct and indirect) cost of dams in sheer economic terms, these are often among the hardest projects to manage, weigh and justify, especially after the fact, since those who are to benefit from such projects are most often also those who end up even deeper in debt; in many cases, these are developing countries that are already in a parlous economic situation. The responsibilities of national authorities when they encumber their citizens with future debts are hard to overestimate, and the connections between state bodies and powerful multinational corporations must be transparent, in order to forestall suspicions of corruption.

Representation is a hot issue in the planning of many damming projects. Whom, for instance, do the international organisations that warn against megadams on rivers like the Nile represent: the local people in need of electricity and water, or the dams' sponsors (who more often than not live in the richer parts of the world)? Who are the stakeholders in a damming case? And indeed who decides who is a stakeholder and who is not? Do the interests of people go hand in hand with the interests of nature, such as in protected areas and national parks? The ideologies and involvement of both authorities and institutions, as well as non-governmental and grass-roots organisations, in the hydropolitics of a dam have to be scrutinised: one must do top-down and bottom-up tracing of ideologies, interests, power and finance.

A truly interdisciplinary enterprise

It is necessary to consider early on that rivers and their catchment landscapes are ecosystems of such importance for the dependent life that any major (or even minor) alterations will always have an impact on the landscape. The life that depends on them includes not only the flora and fauna, but also the millions of humans living near (and indeed far) from their banks: they rely on the river for food, transport, hygiene, spiritual sustenance and other needs that the river fulfils directly and indirectly. In terms of time, the impacts of a dam have to be considered far into the future, as well as in the shorter term. Thus, the mapping and analysis of the hydropolitics of dams is a truly interdisciplinary enterprise. The question of 'what is a river for' always divides people into opposing groups: those for and those against. There is perhaps a third group: those who do not take a stand – but when a symbolic river like the Nile is at stake, few will be able to stand by passively. The bottom line is that damming for various purposes is a complex matter, covering as many intentions and reasons as there are interest groups. Last but not least, the outcomes of dams sometimes differ from the original plans.

A further issue that is connected to, and that stems from, what has already been said is how the present politics and power struggles, ideas and values frame and shape the planning, building and use of dams, whether for hydropower or irrigation. It seems that hydropower is even more controversial when it comes to who benefits and who does not; that said, large-scale irrigation or other water management can also have many aspects that do not always serve those people in whose name the dam was justified. The restrictions on ownership and access to land, water and resources in general are welcomed by some, but resisted by others. On the one hand, the project may be seen as a solution to poverty and underdevelopment; on the other, it may be viewed as the very root of those problems and thus counter to the interests of the public. The background of land and resource rights is very important here – though when dams are on the agenda, it is not always taken into consideration by the political and economic powers. The researcher has to map these carefully. The two biggest groups of players on the damming stage are usually 1) the nation state (represented by its government and institutions), which is seeking foreign investment, industrial development and increased income generally, and 2) other national and/or international companies, which are seeking partners in trade, investment opportunities and the expansion of markets. The ways in which these powerful actors interact with the public, paying attention (or not) to people's multiple voices are of the utmost importance in hydropolitical research.

In many cases, politicians, especially those representing the nation state, will voice arguments that portray the project in the most positive light for all members of the nation, as if it were a unified group of people. Nationalism is a powerful ideology to mobilise public opinion, but it often hides the many and controversial aspects of costly projects like dams. The ties of national politicians to the prospectors and entrepreneurs, financial bodies (both national and international), engineering firms, designers, etc. have to be traced and analysed, especially where corruption is likely and where the power relations between the prospectors, those affected and the recipients of benefits are uneven. Legal frameworks and regulations, sanctions and monitoring of projects are all part of this mapping, not least in the follow-up to damming projects, as the effects of these usually only surface gradually. The bargaining power of stakeholders is crucial for understanding a damming project. Today's increased focus on megaprojects, such as dams and other large-scale engineering projects, will always have to involve national and international companies and institutions, huge sums of money (which often leads to large and long-lasting debts), land-grabbing, and the large-scale migration across continents of workers, who often have few rights and work in unacceptable conditions. Decision making is sometimes non-transparent; accountability in terms of risk and adverse, unexpected consequences is not formalised or even anticipated; and in the end, if something goes wrong, those who have to pick up the pieces are those who are least able.

The issue of development comes to the forefront here, as does the eternal question of who owes what: any national government will have to borrow huge sums of money from foreign financial institutions, whether they are connected to the international development agencies (which have their own development ideologies and agendas) or to private investors. When mapping the flow of finance, the researcher is concerned with more than just the amount of money; equally fascinating is who has an interest in what, how connections are made (even behind the scenes), who will ultimately benefit from the debt, and how all this is presented in the rhetoric, whether public or private, national or corporate. Again, one has to put things into the wider context, and the key question is what the water and/or energy is going to be used for – public consumption, industrial production or both. Often, the electrification of developing nations is not possible without the investment of foreign actors and companies, which are seeking 'green' energy for their products, factories and plants. Thus, the national government will justify the building of a big dam with deals to sell the bulk of the electricity to an economically strong buyer, but will at the same time stress that the public can purchase what is left of the energy. The interconnectedness (and often interdependence) of hydropower dams and industrial development shows how damming projects can never be understood in isolation from other trajectories of industrial and agricultural development. Dams for hydro and irrigation are also closely and inescapably interconnected with infrastructure development, such as transport, communication, sewerage and general water provision, both urban and rural.

An additional and sometimes controversial aspect of hydropower is that it is among the cleanest types of energy available, only bettered by solar and wind power. Now that carbon-based fuels are to be abandoned, states and corporations are more eager than ever to power their production with such 'green' sources. They thus want to portray their products as not harmful to the environment, and so the proponents of a hydropower dam can adduce an important argument. Industrial production such as the refining of alloys is very damaging to ecosystems, pouring highly toxic waste into waterways and soils. It is, nevertheless, portrayed as 'sustainable', 'clean', 'green', 'eco-friendly' and any other term that can be used to launder a dirty product – simply because the process uses hydropower, rather than coal or oil. It has to be noted that hydropower is not CO_2 neutral, as reservoirs often release large amounts of greenhouse gases when forests and other vegetated land are destroyed, even if they subsequently enable land reclamation and re-vegetation elsewhere.

The issue of technology

The technical and technological aspects of dams should also be mentioned, as should the fact that a river is always part of a bigger ecological, geographical and geological landscape – as well as of a political, social and cultural landscape. The design of dams is often seen as the business of specialists, being too complicated for anybody else to deal with or understand. But their architecture should not be left to just a handful of people: these structures often have huge and long-lasting impacts on their surroundings and on the aesthetics of the landscape – cultural, ecological or whatever – to which they belong. The issue of technology has to do with the very practicalities of risk and security; one may, for instance, ask what the possible consequences of megastructures like dams and their connected infrastructure could be. They are sometimes built in areas with unstable geological conditions – even sometimes in active volcanic and earthquake zones – but do we really have the ability to manage potential dangers with technological fixes, as is sometimes claimed?

Other questions that arise include the effects of dams – whether for electric production or irrigation – on groundwater and the hydrology of ecosystems which affect both humans and other inhabitants of human–nature systems, be they animals or plants. The melting and disappearance of the glaciers that feed so many of the earth's rivers affect dams and their management; this in turn has a profound impact on human settlements and urban areas that extend along riverbanks. The confinement of rivers by structures such as buildings, roads and dams is a growing problem, not least because of more extreme precipitation patterns, with floods at one extreme and dry river courses at the other. The buffering effects of wetlands and river estuaries on floods (and droughts) are being removed from the equation, as these ecosystems are altered or eroded, often due to damming. With climate change come stronger and more unpredictable winds, rising sea levels and increased coastal erosion, which all put settlements and ecosystems at even greater threat. The risks to the human presence from these processes, often exacerbated by dams, are sometimes pushed to the side; but those risks are often far more pressing than people generally realise.

Climate change is increasingly to be viewed in the context of damming and water management in general. With rising temperatures, rivers predominantly fed by glaciers (and precipitation in the form of snow and/or rain) will increase their volume, at least for as long as the glaciers last. Once the glaciers are gone, the rivers will only continue to exist if precipitation persists or increases in their catchment area. The potential disappearance of the earth's major rivers in the future is of great concern to many national authorities and international development bodies; but it is scientifically very hard to predict, as knowledge of how precipitation patterns will change is limited. These patterns are coming under close scrutiny in climate change research. Generally, scientists warn of increased extremes: in the intensity and length of precipitation and in its distribution; at the same time, droughts will also increase – sometimes even in the same geographical area. This unpredictability is shedding fresh light on dams, their design, purpose and management. Researchers need to take all this into consideration, since dams are among the longest-lasting human-made structures. Though whether they beat the pyramids, only the distant future will tell.

In an article in *Nature Climate Change*, Declan Conway (2017) presents the latest research on the effects of climate change on the hydrology of the Nile Basin, and es-

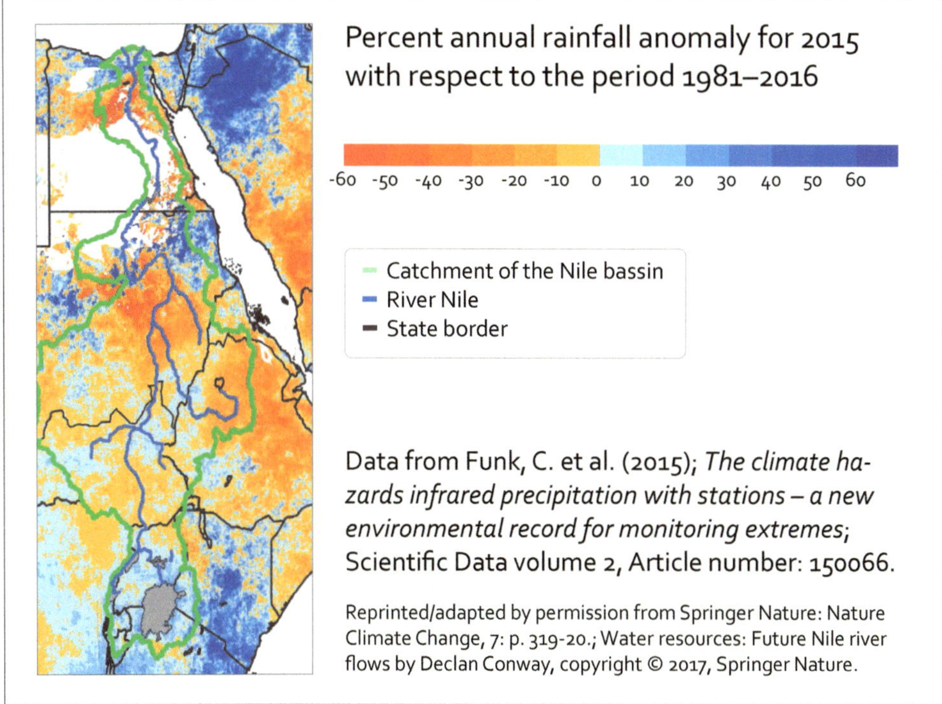

Figure 1.2. Percent annual rainfall anomaly for 2015 with respect to the period 1981–2016.

pecially on precipitation and drought.[1] In general, it looks as though the Nile's annual flow will increase, but so will its variability; this poses a problem for water provision and management for the millions who depend on the river for their livelihood. The biggest problem is that the pattern of rain vs. drought is already (and will increasingly be) rather unpredictable in terms of timing and location; this makes it hard to plan for agriculture, animal husbandry and hydropower production. While people, societies and states in general have for millennia been flexible and resilient in adapting to change, in future they will have to be even more so. Dams can be used as buffers to deal with the increasing and extreme oscillation between the presence and absence of water (both for hydropower and irrigation), if their location and design permit it; but if a dam diverts water to one region, that can mean that water is unavailable in other areas, especially downstream. Thus, the tension between countries over access to Nile water will probably rise, as spells of drought increase in length and intensity, threatening food and power production and security. The increased need for cooperation between the riparian states is evident in the following chapters; otherwise they face more conflict over water. Whatever the reactions are presently, future water scarcity and fluctuations will force the Nile River Basin states somehow to communicate and negotiate – as Conway puts it, 'reinforcing the need for consensus and regional cooperation over Nile waters'.[2]

---

1   Conway (2017)
2   Conway (2017). p. 320.

Case studies and histories of dams in Africa

The following chapters shed light on many of the issues mentioned here in the introduction, bringing frequently abstract descriptions and analyses down to earth (literally) and giving them the life and urgency we need if they are to seem relevant to us – if they are to make us care. The chapters include case studies and histories of dams on the African continent; most of these involve dams on the River Nile, but they possess a much wider geographical appeal and portray a truly overarching picture of the importance of rivers both for human beings and for the nature they live off and in.

Terje Oestigaard introduces the monumental Aswan Dam to the reader in his chapter 'The first Aswan Dam in Egypt – a useful pyramid? Imperialists and archaeologists, cotton and complaints', playing on our ingrained visioning of the pyramids, the Nile and other Egyptian symbols. Each of these instantly evokes the others in our historical imagination – and even if the Aswan Dam is considerably (!) younger than the pyramids and temples of Egypt, many people have drawn parallels between these megastructures – and have even claimed that the dam is superior to the others in importance and engineering ingenuity. Oestigaard tells us the story of the damming of the Nile from ancient times, in various attempts to harness and control its waters; he outlines how it became a central goal of British colonial rule to perfect that project and claims that nothing else mattered in Egypt but the taming of the Nile for irrigation (and thus agriculture). Preserving archaeological sites for the sake of tourism and cultural heritage was overshadowed by the drive to grow cotton for the English textile industries. Oestigaard shows how ideas of 'development' are often to be sought in discourses that originate outside the local setting (even if the locals are the people who, it is claimed, should benefit from projects like dams) – in this case, in the corridors of the colonial power centre, rather than among the Egyptians themselves.

Oestigaard's other chapter, 'A billion-dollar ritual? Spirit appeasement ceremonies behind the Bujagali Dam, Uganda' discusses more recent events in Uganda, surrounding the Bujagali hydropower dam on the White Nile which was inaugurated in 2012. Here, we also hear of cultural values and local vs. national and more global issues and controversies; but this time the actors are more to the forefront, as the author gives us a glimpse of the hydropolitics played out in the media, local encounters and planning reports (among other sources). The question here is ultimately about who has the power to define and decide what is at stake when a dam is built. This intriguing story shows how the actual effects and impacts of a dam, in terms of gigawatts of electricity and millions of dollars, seem almost irrelevant in the context of local people's perceptions, the social and political divides within a country that undertakes megaprojects like dams, and the misconceptions that foreign investors and prospectors can have when alien (to them) customs and values are played out.

In his chapter 'Smallholder-managed large-scale irrigation schemes in Ethiopia', Atakilte Beyene presents a case study of the Koga Dam and irrigation scheme in Ethiopia and considers what insights it gives into the many sides of such a large-scale project: its expected characteristics and outcomes, but also the more unexpected and emerging social, cultural and economic results. Instead of just considering the more technological sides of irrigation and agriculture, the case study reveals how a government manages to tighten its grip on its citizens (in this case, through an irrigation scheme), and how the same scheme simultaneously strengthens cooperation among the large and marginalised group of smallholders in Ethiopia. Here we see how the role of the state in governing and managing different groups and in controlling resources is inseparable from – and indeed determines the outcomes of – a seemingly politically innocuous project like an irrigation scheme. And from the other side – bottom up, so to speak – we see how local groups react in a far from passive and powerless way, although the current situation renders them more dependent on the state than before. When formal policy in the form of bureaucracy meets local realities in the fields, the outcome cannot be predicted; it has to be monitored and analysed as it unfolds. At the root is water, soil, local management systems and people's agency.

Interestingly, Kjell Havnevik has two chapters about the same dam project. As is so often the case with megaprojects, various financial, political and other obstacles once seemed to have consigned a dam to be a mere idea on paper – a dream of development and progress. And then the tide turned and the idea became reality. We kindly ask the reader to bear this in mind. The two chapters on Stiegler's Gorge in Tanzania provide an object lesson on the multi-layered nature of dams. In his earlier chapter 'The dam that was never built: The Stiegler's Gorge project in Tanzania', Havnevik tells the story of the Stiegler's Gorge project, which was to comprise a dam and a reservoir to provide water for a hydropower plant. Though the river in question is not the Nile (as in the other chapters), nevertheless the case sheds interesting light on any dam project, whether for electricity production, irrigation or water storage and management. The fact that at the time of writing the project had not materialised (after a hundred years of planning and negotiation) was hardly unprecedented in the history of megadams; and in tracing the process, Havnevik showed the many economic, political and ideological implications that a complex phenomenon like a dam can have.

In Havnevik's chapter on the more recent project developments, 'The Stiegler's Gorge project in Tanzania: The dam that will be built?', he discusses the latest moves in the history of the dam and the fact that it will at last materialise, since the Tanzanian government recently opened up the tendering process for its construction. The familiar tensions between the different players in dam-building are as great as ever. So will the government lead the way, with the interests of its citizens as a guiding light, and build a multipurpose dam for both energy production and water management for agriculture? Or will the interests of financially strong foreign players, hungry for Africa's natural resources, dictate how and why the dam is designed and operated? Only time will tell; but implementation of the project offers a unique opportunity for a country like Tanzania, with its enormous potential for prosperity – as well as an opportunity for those interested in such historical events as dam-building to observe and learn.

In Ana Elisa Cascão's chapter, 'Storing Nile waters upstream: The hydropolitical implications of dam-building in Sudan and Ethiopia', it becomes clear how complex the system of the Nile is in terms of geography, ecology, hydrology, socio-economics, politics – or indeed from any angle. Her analysis of the history of the Nile's hydropolitics shows how crucial it is to know what led to the present state, in order to begin to imagine how future water requirements can be met, especially in light of increased fluctuations in water provision and storage due to climate change, population increase and global economic pressure on the resource. Not only are those countries important that control the territory where the river rises and where it flows into the sea (although, when the Nile is on the agenda, that is often where the focus lies), but so are the midstream countries, such as Sudan. That country is increasingly claiming its space in the economic development of the region and has a plan for the huge expansion of its irrigation system. Ethiopia is also an upstream player in the competition for water. The third big player is Egypt, with its longstanding leadership in utilising the river for irrigation and hydropower. Considering developments to date, how will these three countries interact in the future, when the Nile's water becomes more and more crucial as the key to food and energy production?

References

Conway, Declan (2017), Water resources: Future Nile river flows, *Nature Climate Change*, 7: 319-20.

Opposite page:
Technical drawing of a dam, April 2013.
Photo: JB Dodane, Flickr.

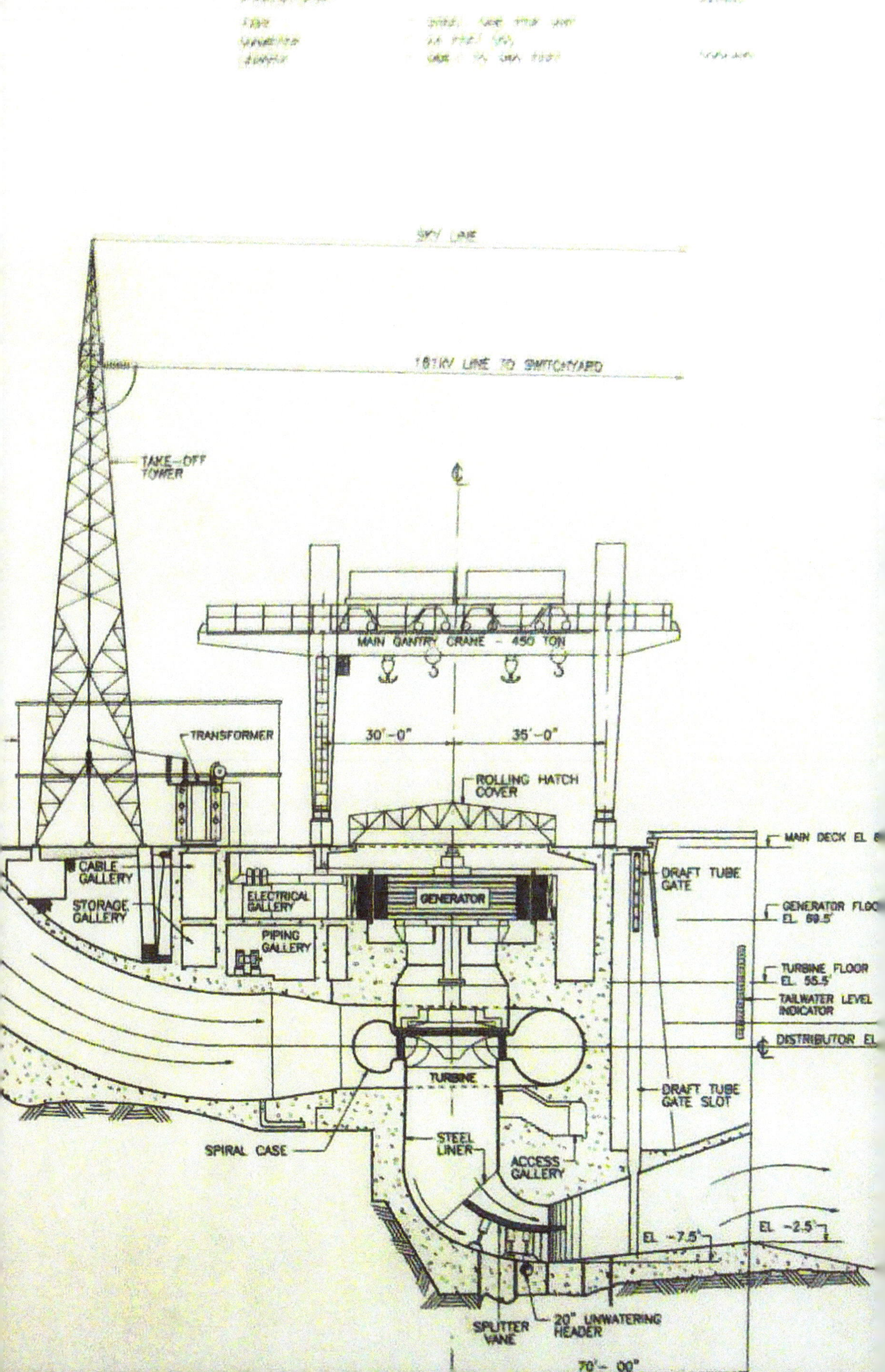
SKY LINE
161KV LINE TO SWITCHYARD
TAKE-OFF TOWER
MAIN GANTRY CRANE - 450 TON
TRANSFORMER
30'-0"
35'-0"
ROLLING HATCH COVER
MAIN DECK EL 8
DRAFT TUBE GATE
GENERATOR FLOOR EL 69.5'
CABLE GALLERY
STORAGE GALLERY
ELECTRICAL GALLERY
GENERATOR
TURBINE FLOOR EL 55.5'
TAILWATER LEVEL INDICATOR
PIPING GALLERY
DISTRIBUTOR EL
SPIRAL CASE
TURBINE
DRAFT TUBE GATE SLOT
STEEL LINER
ACCESS GALLERY
EL -7.5'
EL -2.5'
SPLITTER VANE
20" UNWATERING HEADER
70'-00"

It is remarkable that archaeologists in the late nineteenth century were able to influence the political processes, and to bring about a reduction in the height of the Aswan Dam.

/ Terje Oestigaard, p. 35

The temple of Hathor and Nefertari, also known as the Small Temple, at Abu Simbel in southern Egypt, near the border to Sudan, was relocated in 1960's to prevent them from being submerged during the creation of Lake Nasser and the Aswan High Dam. Photo: Mark Fischer, Flickr.

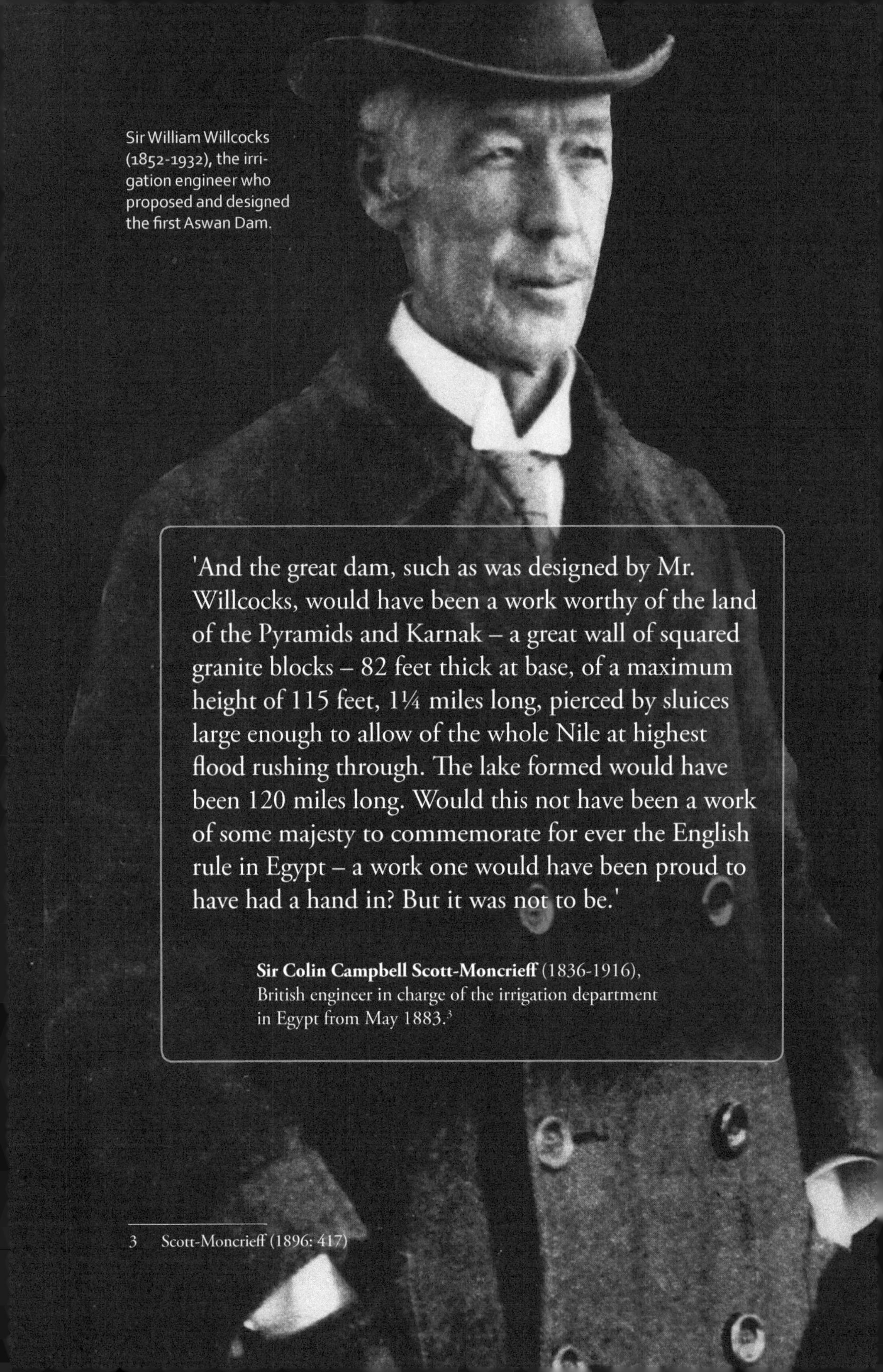

Sir William Willcocks (1852-1932), the irrigation engineer who proposed and designed the first Aswan Dam.

'And the great dam, such as was designed by Mr. Willcocks, would have been a work worthy of the land of the Pyramids and Karnak – a great wall of squared granite blocks – 82 feet thick at base, of a maximum height of 115 feet, 1¼ miles long, pierced by sluices large enough to allow of the whole Nile at highest flood rushing through. The lake formed would have been 120 miles long. Would this not have been a work of some majesty to commemorate for ever the English rule in Egypt – a work one would have been proud to have had a hand in? But it was not to be.'

Sir Colin Campbell Scott-Moncrieff (1836-1916), British engineer in charge of the irrigation department in Egypt from May 1883.[3]

3 Scott-Moncrieff (1896: 417)

CHAPTER 2

The First Aswan Dam in Egypt – a useful pyramid?

Imperialists and archaeologists, cotton and complaints

Terje Oestigaard

The First Aswan Dam, also called the Aswan Low Dam, was an engineering marvel when it was completed in 1902; not only was it the world's largest dam at the time, but it was a fundamental and instrumental part of Britain's imperialism in the Nile Basin. Conventionally, it has been claimed that the British marched upstream because of the 'frontiers of fear'. Terje Tvedt argues that on the one hand, it was the limited nature of the irrigation water in Egypt, and on the other hand, the abundance of Nile waters to be controlled for the benefit of Egypt and cotton production that served as the motive for the imperial strategy.[4] As he asks, why were the British much more interested in the modest White Nile than in the mighty Blue Nile, which provides much more water, and why did they argue that it was just a question of time before they had to occupy Sudan?

The First Aswan Dam was a key to all these questions; but as the quote above shows, the original masterplan for the dam did not at first materialise. The aim of this chapter is therefore to discuss the historical background for the plan and implementation of the dam, and also how archaeologists – for the first time in history – campaigned successfully against a dam, even at the height of British imperialism. Thus, the chapter begins with an archaeological expose, looking at the prehistory of one of the world's oldest dams, which was found in Egypt and probably played a central role in pyramid building. We continue with a historical background and discussion of the role of agriculture in nineteenth-century Egypt and the enormous debts accumulated by the Egyptian *khadif* that had to be paid back. We examine the role of archaeologists campaigning for the protection of the temples at Philae when the Aswan Dam was built, which would have been submerged by the reservoir. And the chapter concludes with a short discussion about the relevance today of understanding the 1902 dam.

---

4   Tvedt 2004; 2011a; 2011b; 2012; 2016

Figure 2.1. Dams or pyramids? The annual inundation of the Nile in relation to the pyramids at Giza. Photo: Lehnert & Landrock 1924.

Dams: The useful pyramids?

Dams have been seen as useful pyramids[5] – a phrasing which implicitly hints that the construction of the massive pyramids was not useful (Figure 2.1). And true, the Aswan High Dam (which opened in 1971), for instance, has been seen as a more awesome structure than the pyramids. In volume, it is 17 times greater than the Great Pyramid at Giza.[6] The importance of the Aswan High Dam was described thus by Nasser in 1958:

> For thousands of years the Great Pyramids of Egypt were foremost among the engineering marvels of the world. They ensured life after death to the Pharaohs. Tomorrow, the gigantic High Dam, more significant and seventeen times greater than the Pyramids, will provide a higher standard of living for all Egyptians.[7]

While the world's oldest dam was not in ancient Egypt, control of water and irrigation was central to the king and the state organisation right from the very foundation of that civilisation. The Scorpion macehead, for instance, which dates to c. 3000 BC, depicts the cutting of an irrigation canal that allows watering of the fields. And the Palermo stone meticulously documented the annual flood from the first dynasties.[8]

---

5   Schnitter 1994
6   Benedick 1979: 123
7   Joesten 1960: 59
8   Oestigaard 2011

The world's oldest dam is probably the Jawa Dam in Jordan, close to the border with Syria. It was about 80 metres in length, with a height of 5 metres, and the total storage potential of the complex (including three other ponds) has been estimated at 42,000 cubic metres.[9] This dam was built late in the fourth millennium BC (around 3500 BC), and not only were there large reservoirs, but also diversion dams and canals that extended over 2 km in length.[10]

Although not *the* oldest, the remains of *one of* the oldest dams in the world were discovered in Egypt in 1885 by Georg Schweinfurth. It is situated in a dry riverbed, Wadi Garawi, at Sadd el-Kafara in Helwan Governorate, and is also known as 'the Barrier of the Pagans', located in the eastern desert some 30 km south of Cairo. Ernest Mackay found several pieces of pottery in an enclosure in the vicinity, which was probably related to huts that accommodated the builders or users of the dam. The form of the pottery remains was characteristic of the Third and the Fourth Dynasties. No pottery of later date was found in the vicinity.[11] In other words, this dam was built at the same time – or perhaps a little earlier – than Khufu's Great Pyramid at Giza!

It is estimated that it took 10–12 years to complete the dam, which was constructed to absorb flash flood waves.[12] The archaeologist G.W. Murray measured the dam: its crest was about 108 metres long, and its height from the lowest point on the riverbed was about 12 metres. The structure consisted of two separate dams with a loose stone filling. Each wall was about 24 metres thick at the base, and the space between them at ground level was approximately 36 metres. This space was filled with a combination of shingle from the wadi bed and rubble from the hillsides. Thus the total thickness of the dam base was no less than 84 metres. This was a colossal architectural structure.[13]

An approximately 3 kilometre path from the dam led to a large alabaster quarry, situated at the head of the valley.[14] Most likely, the blocks of alabaster were brought to the mouth of the valley, either pulled by donkeys or swung from poles carried by men, because in several places the path was very narrow, making it impossible to use sleds. The river could have been used to transport the blocks at certain times of the year, but this seems unlikely, since the blocks would have had to be lifted right over the dam at the end of the journey, or up to the level ground of the ravine's southern side.[15]

The purpose of this dam is as intriguing as its huge size and antiquity. Murray (1947) estimated its capacity at about 575,000 cubic metres. For his calculations, Murray used contemporary rainfall records (which he assumed to be quite similar to those in antiquity): during the period 1904-1944, there were 29 occasions on which 10 mm or more of rain fell on a single day, and 10 occasions of more than 20 mm. The catchment area is 185 square kilometres, and a natural runoff of 1 mm corresponds to

---

9   Fahlbusch 2007: 77
10   Braemer et al. 2009: 47. Brown and Jackson 2017.
11   Mackay 1915: 39; Petrie and Mackay 1915: 38; Hellström 1952: 424
12   Garbrecht 1985
13   Murray 1947; Hellström 1952: 424
14   Mackay 1915: 39
15   Mackay 1915: 40

a volume of 185,000 cubic metres. With rainfall of 20 mm (which, as we have said, occurs about 10 times in 40 years at Helwan), 8 mm would have been absorbed immediately, and a quarter of the remaining rainfall would have created some 500,000 or 600,000 tonnes of water flowing through the wadi, filling the reservoir and causing the dam to overflow.[16]

After the first heavy rainfall it faced, then, the dam filled up and – intriguingly – collapsed. There are no traces of silt deposits, which means that it must have fractured very soon after construction. This disaster had a severe impact on the Ancient Egyptians' notions of taming the waters, and the failure of this major project was not soon forgotten: there were no attempts in Egypt to build dams for another 4,500 years.[17]

It is uncertain why the dam was built in the first place. Schweinfurth surmised that its purpose was to provide fresh water to the workers at the alabaster quarry upstream of the dam;[18] but such a monumental construction project just to provide water to quarry workers does not seem very convincing. Fahlbusch has come up with another interesting hypothesis. As a papyrus document testifies, during the Old Kingdom, huge stones for construction purposes were transported on sleds over damp mud roads, formed of sediment from the Nile. The transportation of these massive alabaster blocks to the Nile would have necessitated a mud road approximately 2 metres wide and 50 centimetres thick; the dam may have been built for this purpose – although the water necessary to construct such a road would have amounted only to about 10 per cent of its capacity.[19]

More than 4,500 years later, it was the British who proposed to build a new dam in Egypt; but this time it had a completely different economic purpose and political background.

'The Egyptian question is the irrigation question'

Samuel Baker (1821-1893), who served as Governor-General of the Equatorial Nile Basin (today's South Sudan and Northern Uganda) between 1869 and 1873, embarked on several exploration tours to the Nile Basin area and the interior of central Africa, for example exploring the Atbara river and other Nile tributaries. William Garstin (1849-1925), the leading British water engineer along the Nile at the turn of the century, wrote about Baker in 1909, 16 years after his death:

> Sir Samuel Baker left a reputation behind him, in Central Africa – throughout every region in which he travelled – that has hardly been equalled, and has certainly never been surpassed ... He was of the best type of Englishman, and made the name of England greater, wherever he went, by the impress of his just and manly character.[20]

---

16 Murray 1955: 174
17 Hellström 1952: 430; Garbrecht 1985
18 Hellström 1952: 424
19 Fahlbusch 2009
20 Garstin (1909: 126)

Figure 2.2. Aswan today. Photo Terje Oestigaard.

Moreover, continued Garstin, there are two remarkable aspects to Baker's accounts of his travels. First, there is the accuracy of his descriptions; but more importantly from a political perspective, there is his foresight with regard to the future control and development of the Nile. Baker was the first to suggest building dams at the northern cataracts, in order to store water for cultivation in Egypt.[21] While the importance of the flood was emphasised, as Baker wrote in 1867:

> The lake-sources of Central Africa support the *life* of Egypt, by supplying a stream, throughout all seasons … These rivers [the Blue Nile and Atbara], although streams of extreme grandeur during the period of the Abyssinian rains, from the middle of June until September, are reduced during the dry months to utter insignificance; the Blue Nile becoming so shallow as to be unnavigable, and the Atbara perfectly dry.

He concludes: 'It may thus be stated: The equatorial lakes feed Egypt; but the Abyssinian rivers *cause the inundation*'.[22] Baker's suggestion in the 1860s of building a dam at Aswan was ahead of its time; but only a few decades later, it was a central part of developments in the early British Nile Empire.

Perennial irrigation was introduced and developed by the great moderniser, Muhammed Ali (1805-1848) and his successors. It revolutionised agriculture, increasing and multiplying its surpluses. Muhammed Ali once said: 'Give me regulators at the heads of canals, and I am master of Egypt'.[23] In fact, he was apparently so eager to

---

21   Garstin 1909: 126-27
22   Baker 1867: viii–x
23   Allen 1983: 471

construct barrages in the delta without incurring any delays that he wanted a French engineer to dismantle the Giza Pyramids, in order to secure the necessary building material.[24] Fortunately, the engineer obtained the necessary materials elsewhere. Ismail Pasha (1830-1895) continued the agricultural policies, and after 1882 the British built extensively on them.

When Ismail Pasha became Viceroy of Egypt in 1863, the country's debt was 3 million pounds; when he was deposed in 1879, the country was bankrupt and in debt to the tune of 91 million pounds.[25] Ismail wanted to modernise Egypt, but that came at a high price: borrowed money. In 1877, Ismail said in an interview: 'My country is no longer African; we now form part of Europe'.[26] The borrowed money financed schools and infrastructure, modernisation projects and the Suez Canal, but also lavish personal spending. An obituary of Ismail Pasha wrote:

> ... for fifteen years [he] gave a loose rein to his extravagant taste for display and self-indulgence, without wholly neglecting his duties as a ruler. He built railways, made ports at Alexandria, Port Said and Suez, opened the Suez Canal, and extended his dominion to the equator; but the vast wealth which came into his hands, through the rise in the price of cotton caused by the American civil war and from numerous Egyptian loans, was squandered for the most part in reckless prodigality.[27]

His unfinished Giza Palace was furnished with moth-eaten French hangings and curtains, and in the government archives there was even an order for 100 pianos for the ladies of the harem.[28] 'How far the money borrowed was wasted; what proportion was spent for the good of the country, it is impossible to discover. Such was the chaos of the accounts!'.[29]

In his *The River Nile in the Age of the British* (2004), Tvedt analyses in detail how British imperial policies in the Nile had one overarching aim: to secure British interests. Britain took control of Egypt in 1882. Small quantities of cotton produced in the delta were sold into a growing world market from the 1820s, but from the 1860s onwards cotton exports made up about 80 per cent of Egypt's exports. British industry had huge economic interests in Egypt. The Lancashire textile mills aimed to reduce their dependence on American cotton and increase the supply of cheaper Egyptian cotton. To increase productivity (and hence profits), more Nile water was needed at the right time – Egypt's summer. This came before the Blue Nile's annual floods, and therefore cotton production was dependent on the waters of the White Nile. The overriding question was how to secure enough water for cotton production, and at the same

---

24 Sandes 1937: 363
25 Although British pounds sterling and Egyptian pounds were not identical, in 1914, for instance, the Egyptian pound was on a par with the pound sterling, standing at £1.026; see Hansen 1983: 868, fn. 5
26 Bowen 1886: 330, fn. 1
27 Obituary: Ismail Pasha, Journal of the American Geographical Society of New York, 27/1 (1895): 85.
28 Sandes 1937: 371
29 Dawkins 1901: 496

time control the potentially devastating floods.[30] Thus, by the end of the nineteenth century, 'increased and improved water control was destined to top the agenda of any administration in Egypt'.[31]

The British were the first to truly see and to try to exploit this connection, and the colonisation cannot be understood properly without a water perspective emphasising the Nile as a river system. The British administration under Lord Cromer understood this from the very outset, and British policy was structured around the Nile. In his imperial strategy, he wrote: 'When, eventually, the waters of the Nile, from the Lakes to the sea, are brought fully under control, it will be possible to boast that Man, in this case the Englishman, has turned the gifts of Nature to the best possible advantage.' Arguing in favour of the construction of the Aswan Dam, Cromer wrote that it is of 'utmost importance' because 'the prosperity of Egypt depends wholly on the Nile'. In a letter to Prime Minister Salisbury, he emphasised again: 'There can be no doubt that the most crying want of the country at present is an increase in the water supply'.[32]

That famous phrase 'Egypt is the gift of the Nile' is ascribed to Herodotus. But in fact, most probably it stems from Hecataeus of Miletus, who travelled through Egypt almost a century before Herodotus.[33] Some 2,500 years later, it was said: 'To draw up a list of Egypt's economic resources is almost to damn with faint praise, so little has she to boast of aside from her agricultural possibilities'.[34] According to Scott-Moncrieff, the Nile's water was fundamental: 'Its [Egypt's] unique position is due to the benefits it [the Nile] confers on Egypt in turning it from being a desert into being the richest of agricultural lands, supporting with ease a population of about six hundred to the square mile'.[35] Controlling the Nile was thus of vital importance to Britain, and the British decision to occupy the Upper Nile can be seen as an example of a far-sighted imperial expansionist policy, driven by a complex mixture of economic and political considerations framed by the geographical and hydrological characteristic of the Nile, according to Tvedt, who further argues that the British had 'become rulers of a truly hydraulic society, where stability and wealth depended upon the water of the Nile'.[36]

The then Egyptian Prime Minister Nubar Pasha (1884-1888 and 1894-1895) summarised Egypt's situation and position in a famous one-liner: 'The Egyptian question is the irrigation question'.[37] British banks also had a strong interest in the Egyptian economy. In 1882, Egypt's foreign debt had increased to 100 million pounds, with an annual debt amounting to 5 million pounds, of which a large part went to Britain. The 'Nile water awareness' in London was so great that The Times reported regularly on the Nile's water discharges.[38] Alongside the Suez Canal, it was vital in making agricul-

---

30   Tvedt 2004: 20-22
31   Tvedt 2004: 22
32   Tvedt 2011a: 182-83
33   Darby et al. 1977: 32
34   Gemmill 1928: 299
35   Scott-Moncrieff 1896: 408
36   Tvedt 2011b: 82
37   Tvedt 2011a: 176
38   Tvedt 2011a: 177

ture and cotton exports profitable. Improvements to the irrigation systems were also financed by British loans, and 'for a country which had ruined itself by borrowing, to borrow yet another million under no compulsion, but while still deeply entangled in a financial slough, seemed on the face of it a last imprudence'.[39]

But improving the irrigation schemes in Egypt was part of a greater plan. As Scott-Moncrief argued:

> Supposing that they [the Italians] occupied Khartoum, the first thing they would naturally and very properly do would be to spread the waters of the Low Nile over the Soudan; and no nation in Europe understands irrigation so well. And what would then become of Egypt's cotton crops? They could only be secured by a series of the most costly dams over the river, and the fate of Philæ would surely be sealed.

But he went further: a civilised nation should build dams as far south as the outlet of Lake Victoria. He concluded: 'Is it not evident then, that the Nile from the Victoria Nyanza to the Mediterranean should be under one rule?'.[40]

William Garstin, the leading British water engineer along the Nile, wrote that if they succeeded in taming the Nile, it would be an achievement on a par with the building of the pyramids.[41] The role of the imperial administration and cotton was summed up this way from the British perspective: 'to see the extent to which the whole prosperity of the country is bound up in the cotton crop it is only necessary to note that the population has increased from 6,813,000 in 1882 to 11,189,000 in 1907. This increase is partly due to good government, partly to the great development of irrigation and cotton'.[42]

The Aswan Dam

Scott-Moncrieff took charge of the irrigation department in Egypt in May 1883, and according to himself, 'happy is the reformer who finds things so bad that he cannot make a movement without making an improvement'.[43] According to him:

> Another function of the river is to promote industry by the employment of its water power. We know how valuable is this power even in England, and how much more in countries like Switzerland … And may we not prophesy that some day in the future, when that long stretch of Nubian cataracts has fallen into civilized hands, and when we know how to transmit electric energy with economy, that then our descendants will draw wealth to Egypt from its chains of barren cataracts?[44]

---

39   Dawkins 1901: 502
40   Scott-Moncrieff 1896: 418
41   Tvedt 2011a: 182
42   McFarlane 1909: 381
43   Scott-Moncrieff 1896: 414
44   Scott-Moncrieff 1896: 407

Figure 2.3. Flooding at the Temple of Isis at Philae, an island in the reservoir of the First Aswan Dam. Photo by H.W. Dunning, 1905.

The Aswan Dam, as designed by Willcocks in the 1890s, would partially submerge the temples on the Island of Philae (Figure 2.3). When plans were proposed to submerge the temple, it resulted in an outburst of rage and indignation in London during the summer of 1894. And for the first time since Britain occupied Egypt in 1882, educated opinion in England and France agreed: England should not commit such vandalism. As Scott-Moncrieff wrote: 'In vain it was answered that the place belonged to Egypt, not to England – that the Egyptian, who was to gain so much by the dam, cared absolutely nothing about Ptolemy and his temples – that he was prepared to pay a large price for a great work to benefit his country. What business was it of England to forbid him?' [45]

There were complaints both within and beyond archaeological circles. In London, this letter was presented by an archaeologist:

> I would earnestly call the attention of the archaeological world to this "unavoidable" act of vandalism. It is not enough to say that a committee of three engineers from England, France and Italy has been appointed to study the question: they were not sent in the interest of art, but to study the stability of the dam. I do not wish for a moment to suggest that these three eminent hydraulic engineers are themselves vandals. Yet it is well known that engineers, when swayed by the interests of their calling, do not take into consideration the art side of the question; and it is not to them that we would naturally turn when we want to preserve a world-famous monument, but to men of taste and archaeological knowledge. [46]

45   Scott-Moncrieff 1896: 417
46   Frothingham 1894: 259

The Egyptologist Francis Griffith wrote in 1894:

> There is, however, a black cloud overhead which threatens to burst immediately and utterly destroy the harvest we hoped for from the land of Lower Nubia. Whatever alleviation of the calamity may be effected by the Government and by private surveys and excavation of the threatened ground, the Aswan dam will be the cause of a more rapid and whole sale destruction of antiquities than has ever before been known; and, as such, it must be contemplated with horror by all Egyptologists, to whom this year is likely to be one of painful memory.[47]

The Government was upset with the archaeologists. Scott-Moncrieff said: 'The Egyptians saw no objections to it. The money could be found. But there was an insuperable obstacle created when, on the Island of Philæ, about 250 BC, Ptolemy II built a temple to Isis'.[48] As Willcocks said, 'If the dam be made at Aswan, the temple must either be raised, removed or submerged'.[49] He suggested re-siting it, and he even allowed 250,000 Egyptian pounds for the removal of the temple to another island. Willcocks also suggested to his former chief, Scott-Moncrieff, that the cost of the dam could be financed by selling the Philae temples to the Americans! These plans did not materialise. In the end, the Government surrendered by reducing the level of the reservoir and hence saving the temple.[50]

The result was that the 'majestic structure' (the dam) was reduced by 27 feet and would only be 88 feet high, and hence the Philæ would not be drowned but would remain in a lake. 'Personally I accept the situation,' Scott-Moncrieff wrote, 'for I never believed it would be sacrificed. But as an engineer, I must sigh over the lost opportunity for England of making such a splendid reservoir. And as a friend of Egypt, I sigh still more that the country will not have such a splendid supply of water'.[51] Winston Churchill, on the other hand, was furious that the water reservoir would be reduced to 1 billion cubic metres. 'The State must struggle and the people starve,' he said, 'in orders that professors may exult and tourists find some places on which to scratch their names'.[52]

The construction of the dam began in the winter of 1898 and was completed by the end of

Figure 2.4. Winston Churchill at the age of 30 in 1904. Photo: Imperial War Museum.

47   Griffith 1893–94: 8
48   Scott-Moncrieff 1896: 417
49   Willcocks 1913a: 685
50   Sandes 1937: 382
51   Scott-Moncrieff 1896: 417-18
52   Sandes 1937: 383

Figure 2.5. The First Aswan Dam. The dam from the west bank looking east, 6 December 1901. Photo from Grace's Guide to British Industrial History.

1902 (Figure 2.5). The rapids had a total fall of about 5 metres. The original plan was to make a reservoir at 118 metres above sea level, which would contain 3.7 billion cubic metres of water; but because of the temple, the dam's reservoir was first constructed at 106 metres above sea level. The 1902 dam, with a reservoir height of 106 metres, could only store 1.065 billion cubic metres of water, or less than a third of the original plan.[53]

The archaeologists may have won the opening battle, but it turned out that there was too little water for irrigation. Writing just after completion of the dam in 1902 (when it was likely that the dam would be raised by 6 metres), Griffith challenged Lord Cromer, who, in a parliamentary report, had claimed that archaeology had benefited from the dam:

> We fear that archaeologists, while gratefully acknowledging the care which has been expended by the Government on the monuments at Philae, will hardly acquiesce in the opinion expressed that "the interests of archaeology have gained rather than suffered from the construction of the Assouan dam," except only in regards to the clearance of rubbish from the temple buildings and their safeguarding from gradual ruin. The mere fact that the Nile now soaks miles upon miles of fresh ground teeming with unworked archaeological remains of a perishable character, must itself be a disaster to archaeology, however vast the gain may be to modern Egypt.[54]

---

53   Williams 1912: 44
54   Griffith 1903-04: 20-21

Neither in the short run nor in the long term could archaeology and tourism stand up against imperial policy and economic development. In 1912, the Aswan Dam was raised to 113 metres above sea level. Still, there was not enough water, as Willcocks argues, and 'the true solution was to raise the dam to R.L. [relative level] 118˙00 metres, as originally planned, and impound 4 milliards of cubic metres of water; or even to raise to R.L. 120˙00 metres and impound 5 milliards. To stop at R.L. 113˙00 and impound less than 2½ was short-sighted'.[55]

The total cost, including the raised 1912 reservoir, was £4,220,000. The first dam, completed in 1902 with a reservoir height of 106 metres above sea level, had cost £2,440,000.[56] Despite the high cost, the value of the dam could not be overestimated for either the British or the Egyptians. The Aswan Dam recouped its cost in just one season. In 1902, the flood was very low, but with the water stored in the dam, crops worth USD 2,500,000 were saved and sold.[57] Within ten years of completion of the First Aswan Dam, the total value of Egypt's imports had more than doubled (from 11,000,000 Egyptian pounds to 22,000,000); its exports had increased in value from 13,000,000 Egyptian pounds to 24,000,000; and the country's revenue had increased by 3,500,000 Egyptian pounds. And behind these figures, irrigation was credited as the main driver of progress.[58]

Still, there was not enough water. Initially it was estimated that 4 billion cubic metres of water were necessary for perennial irrigation.[59] The British Empire could build dams, but as it was pointed out:

> British control is complete, however, only up to a certain point. Unaffected by the political manoeuvrings of the ages, the Nile has continued supreme in the economic sphere … British brains and British capital can extend agriculture … But they cannot make of Egypt anything but an agricultural country – they cannot lessen her dependence upon the Nile.[60]

The need for more water continued to increase. A second height extension was begun in 1929 and completed in 1934. By increasing the height by 9 metres, the reservoir's capacity was increased to 5.67 billion cubic metres, or more than 5.5 times the original (1902) amount, with the consequence that the Philae temples were almost submerged.[61]

The inadequacy of the volume of water that it was possible to store and control at Aswan was central to the British expansion and colonisation southwards, to include Sudan and the later development of the Gezira Scheme. The Nile Waters Agreement of 1929 was partly the result of development of the irrigation schemes on the Gezira plain in Sudan, which would become the world's largest cotton farm. However, if Sudan was

---

55 Willcocks 1913a: 740-741
56 Willcocks 1913a: 745
57 Gemmill 1928: 302
58 Willcocks 1913b
59 Sandes 1937: 380
60 Gemmill 1928: 312
61 Sandes 1937: 384-85

going to develop, it needed more water, and quarrels with Egypt over the Nile were unavoidable. The Sennar Dam, which provided water to the Gezira Scheme, was completed in 1925.[62] The use of Nile water was fundamental to Britain's colonial policy to control Egypt. On 22 November 1924, Lord Allenby announced his famous Nile ultimatum: 'The Sudan Government will increase the area to be irrigated in the Gezira from 300,000 feddans to an unlimited figure as need may require'.[63] This statement infuriated the Egyptian public, and Allenby was asked to revoke the ultimatum. After an exchange of notes, the British government committed itself to guaranteeing Egypt's future water supplies by compensating it for the water taken at Sennar, leading to the Nile Waters Agreement of 1929.

Conclusion

Scott-Moncrieff lamented in 1896 that the 'work of some majesty … was not to be'. He was wrong. Less than two decades later, the Aswan Dam had been raised; and it was then raised once more, in 1934. Still, it was insufficient to meet Egypt's demands.

When, in 1971, the Aswan High Dam was inaugurated, with its storage capacity of two annual floods, Egypt's water security was ensured within Egypt's borders. Still, 'Although the dam changed the Nile's behaviour in Egypt, it did not liberate the country and the political actors from the power of the structure of the water system itself. The dam made the Egyptians more dependent on the Nile than ever before'.[64] And as with the First Aswan Dam, archaeology and the Philae temple were once again in the spotlight, together with the Abu Simbel temple – all of which were relocated as part of a UNESCO campaign.

From the First Aswan Dam onwards, there has been opposition to large dams.[65] In a historical perspective, it is remarkable that archaeologists in the late nineteenth century were able to influence the political processes, and to bring about a reduction in the height of the Aswan Dam – at the very peak of the British Empire's imperial and colonial expansion and policy. Today, dam-building in Sudan is in the forefront of disputes between government and archaeologists – and archaeology and indigenous or local people are most often on the losing side. At the core of the debates – a point that Churchill so poignantly emphasised – is the question of what is better for whom, and who can decide for others. Then as now, there is an increasing demand and pressure on water as an ever-scarcer resource. And in particular dam-building highlights the different development aims, strategies and priorities. More often than not, archaeology (or cultural heritage) is at the epicentre of these conflicts (see also chapter 4).

Lastly, there are certain other general aspects that are clearly exemplified by the First Aswan Dam. First, in many places there is an ever-increasing need for more water

---

62   Tvedt 2004: 105-109
63   Tvedt 2004: 110
64   Tvedt and Coopey 2010: 16
65   See, for instance, Oestigaard 2015

and expansion of large-scale water infrastructure. This ties in with the second point: even if the plans are temporarily postponed for political or other reasons (including anti-dam activism), it is always possible (and sometimes fairly easy) to re-engage the dam-building and reactivate cancelled plans (see chapters 5, 6 and 7). Thirdly, loans and debts have to be repaid. Today, the major developments and large-scale water infrastructure projects are funded by foreign money (in the past often by the World Bank; today largely by China). Such massive investments will, of necessity, shape future political and economic debts.

References

Allen, J.A. (1983), Some phases in extending the cultivated area in the nineteenth and twentieth centuries in Egypt, *Middle Eastern Studies*, 19/4: 470-481.

Baker, S.W. (1867), *The Nile Tributaries of Abyssinia, and the Sword Hunters of the Hamran Arabs*. Macmillan and Co., London.

Benedick, R.E. (1979), The High Dam and the transformation of the Nile, *Middle East Journal*, 33/2: 19-44.

Bowen, J.E. (1886). The conflict of East and West in Egypt, *Political Science Quarterly*, 1/2: 295-335.

Braemer, F. et al. (2009), Long-term management of water in the Central Levant: The Hawran Case (Syria), *World Archaeology*, 41/1: 36-57.

Brown, J. Guthrie & Jackson, Donald C. (2017). Encyclopædia Britannica, article on 'Dam', online edition; https://www.britannica.com/technology/dam-engineering#ref984113 (accessed 20 June 2017).

Darby, L., P. Ghalioungui & L. Grivetti (1977), Food: *The gift of Osiris, Volume 1*. Academic Press, London.

Dawkins, C.E. (1901), The Egyptian public debt, *North American Review*, 173/539: 487-507.

Fahlbusch, H. (2007), Water and its use in early history. In J.L. Lozán, H. Grassl, P. Hupfer, L. Menzel & C.-D. Schönwiese (eds), *Global Change: Enough water for all?* Wissenschaftliche Auswertungen, Hamburg, pp. 77-82.

Fahlbusch, H. (2009), Early dams, *Proceedings of the Institution of Civil Engineers*, 162, February, Issue EHI: 13-18.

Frothingham, A.L. (1894), Archaeological news, *American Journal of Archaeology and of the History of the Fine Arts*, 9/2: 229-330.

Garbrecht, G. (1985), Sadd-el-Kafara: The world's oldest large dam, *Water Power & Dam Construction*, July: 71-76.

Garstin, W. (1909), Fifty years of Nile exploration, and some of its results. *Geographical Journal*, 33/2: 117-147.

Gemmill, P.F. (1928), Egypt is the Nile, *Economic Geography*, 4/3: 295-312.

Griffith, F. (1893–94), Hieroglyphic studies &c., *Archaeological Report* (Egypt Exploration Fund): 8-28.

Griffith, F. (1903–04), Archaeology, hieroglyphic studies, etc., *Archaeological Report* (Egypt Exploration Fund): 18-59.

Hansen, B. (1983), Interest rates and foreign capital in Egypt under British occupation, *Journal of Economic History*, 43/4: 867-884.

Hellström, B. (1952), Le plus vieux barrage du monde, *Extrait de la houille blanche*, No. 3: 424-430.

Joesten, J. (1960), Nasser's daring dream: The Aswan High Dam, *World Today*, 16/2: 55-63.

Mackay, E. (1915), Old Kingdom dam in Wadi Gerrawy. In W.M.F. Petrie and E. Mackay, *Heliopolis, Kafr Ammar and Shurafa*. School of Archaeology in Egypt, London, pp. 38-40.

McFarlane, J. (1909), The production of cotton in Egypt, *Journal of the Royal African Society*, 8/32: 372-382.

Murray, G.W. (1947), A note on the el-Kafara; the ancient dam in the Wadi Garawi, *Bulletin de l'institut d'Egypte*, XXVIII, Session 1945-1946. Le Caire.

Murray, G.W. (1955), Water from the desert: Some Ancient Egyptian achievements, *Geographical Journal*, 121/2: 171-181.

Oestigaard, T. (2011), *Horus' eye and Osiris' efflux: The Egyptian civilisation of inundation ca. 3000-2000 BCE*. Archaeopress, Oxford.

Oestigaard, T. (2015), *Dammed divinities: The water powers at Bujagali Falls, Uganda*, Current African Issues, No. 62. Nordic Africa Institute, Uppsala.

Petrie, F. and Mackay, E. (1915), *Heliopolis, Kafr, Ammarand Shurafa*. British School of Archaeology in Egypt, London.

Sandes, E.W.C. (1937), *The Royal Engineers in Egypt and the Sudan*. The Institution of Royal Engineers, Chatham, London.

Schnitter, N.J. (1994), *A History of Dams: The useful pyramids*. A.A. Balkema, Rotterdam.

Scott-Moncrieff, C. (1896), *The Nile, Notices of the Proceedings at the Meetings of the Members of the Royal Institution of Great Britain, with Abstracts and Discourses delivered at the Evening Meetings, Volume XIV, 1883-1885*: 405-418. William Clowes and Sons Limited, London.

Tvedt, T. (2004), *The River Nile in the Age of the British: Political ecology and the quest for economic power*. London: I.B. Tauris.

Tvedt, T. (2011a), Hydrology and empire: The Nile, water imperialism and the partition of Africa, *Journal of Imperial and Commonwealth History*, 39/2: 173-194.

Tvedt, T. (2011b), Water: A source of wars or a pathway to peace? An empirical critique of dominant schools of thought regarding water and geopolitics. In T. Tvedt, G. Chapman and R. Hagen (eds), *A History of Water, Series 2, Vol. 3: Water and Geopolitics in the New World Order*. I.B. Tauris, London.

Tvedt, T. (2012), *Nilen – historiens elv*. Aschehoug, Oslo.

Tvedt, T. (2016), *Water and Society: Changing perceptions of societal and historical development*. I.B. Tauris, London.

Tvedt, T. and R. Coopey (2010), A 'water systems' perspective on history. In T. Tvedt and R. Coopey (eds), *A History of Water, Series 2, Vol. 2: From Early Civilizations to Modern Times*. I.B. Tauris, London.

Willcocks, W. (1913a), *Egyptian Irrigation. Third Edition. Volume I*. E. & F.N. Spon, London.

Willcocks, W. (1913b). *Egyptian Irrigation. Third Edition. Volume II*. E. & F.N. Spon, London.

Williams, A. (1912), *The Romance of Modern Engineering*. Seeley, Service & Co. Limited, London.

While the role of the state in the management of irrigation infrastructure continues to be strong and indispensable, there is a realisation that canal and water management should be transferred to the users.

/ Atakilte Beyene, p.56

Ribb Dam under construction, Amhara state, Ethiopia, October 2014. Photo: Beatrice Mosello ODI.

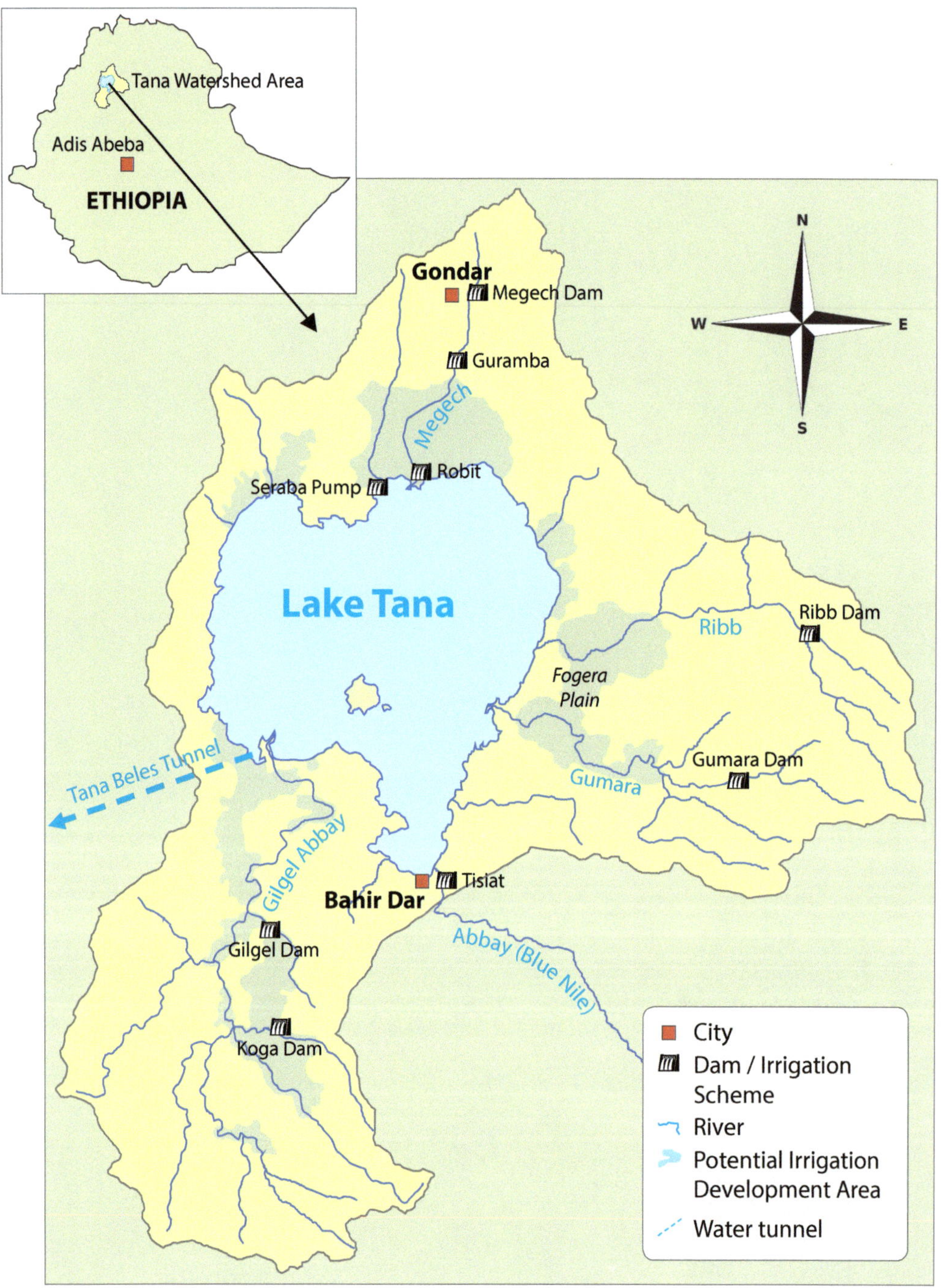

Figure 3.1. Lake Tana Watershed Area. Illustration: Henrik Alfredsson, the Nordic Africa Institute.

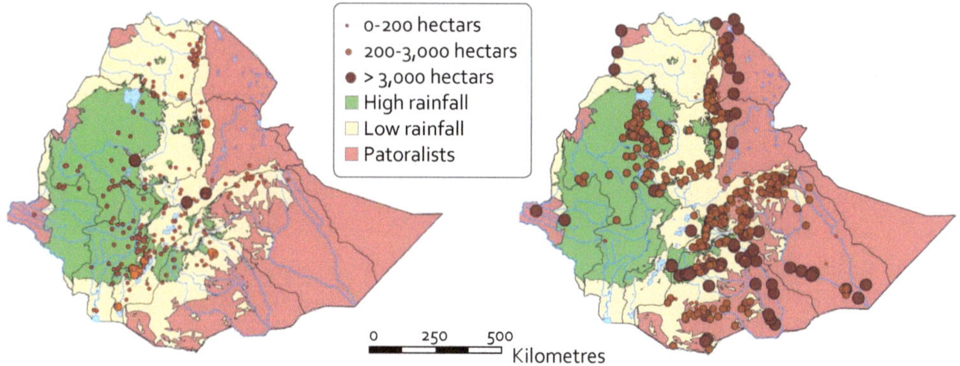

Figure 3.2. Existing irrigation development.
Source: IWMI in Awulachew, S. (2010)

Figure 3.3. Irrigation potential.
Source: IWMI in Awulachew, S. (2010)

CHAPTER 3
Smallholder-managed large-scale irrigation schemes in Ethiopia

Atakilte Beyene

Over the past two decades, water has increasingly become central to Ethiopia's policy and development agenda. Three major policy spheres in which water is key are poverty reduction, economic growth, and climate change mitigation and adaptation objectives. Since the early 2000s, the country has had a political plan for poverty reduction.[66] Under this plan, water harvesting is a main pillar of the national food security strategy. Accordingly, extensive pro-poor, rural and natural resources development programmes have been undertaken in many parts of the country, where rural people have been mobilised for conservation work to reclaim environmentally degraded areas.[67] The construction of small-scale water conservation structures in hillside areas and on arable land forms part of the programme. Similarly, household-level on-farm water-storage facilities, such as ponds, and community-level medium-scale dams are being constructed for irrigation, livestock and other purposes.

---

66   MoFED 2006
67   Gebregziabher 2009

Ethiopia's ambition to achieve middle-income country status by 2025 is also directly or indirectly dependent on water. *The Growth and Transformation Plan* (GTP) of the country, which has been running since 2010, aims to achieve this goal.[68] According to this goal, agricultural growth through improved productivity is conceived as the basis for the transformation. Again, water and land are key to the plan. In addition to the extensive small-scale water development projects, large-scale water infrastructure projects have increasingly become a priority under the GTPs. The economic growth and transformation agenda also embraces the development of commercial and export-oriented agriculture. Notable in this are floriculture, sugar and food production systems; the public and private sectors have been prominent in these production sectors. Since 2008, water and land have been at the heart of a 'new' economic and political discourse. To encourage and attract investors – and thereby the flow of foreign direct investment – into the country, water-rich and high-potential agricultural areas are used as incentives.[69] Although it is not yet completely clear where such investments are situated, many are believed to be located around lakes and along the major water basins of the country, where water is available. Furthermore, historical, political and demographic dynamics in the region are also reinforcing the centrality of water for Ethiopia.[70]

Ethiopia's climate policy – *Climate-Resilient Green Economy* – aims for the country to achieve climate-resilient and green middle-income economic status by 2025, with zero net emissions.[71] Two of the four pillars of the strategy – adoption of improved agriculture and forest land-use measures; and deployment of renewable and clean power generation – relate directly to water.[72] The first calls for an expansion of access and more efficient use of water in agricultural systems. Expansion of small-, medium- and large-scale irrigation schemes is one major area of state intervention. Renewable energy production has also entered a new era, as the country strives to generate the lion's share of its energy needs from hydropower, for which large-scale dams are required.

These broader political, economic and environmental processes have situated water as a key resource, attracting a wide range of actors, such as the state, farmers and investors (domestic and foreign alike). The concurrent expansion of infrastructure surrounding water generates a range of political, social, organisational and environmental processes. Knowledge of the evolving social, institutional and governance system is important, in order to explore the potentials and challenges of the emerging water schemes.

This chapter explores a specific form of state intervention, namely large-scale irrigation constructed by the government for use by smallholder farmers. This type of irrigation is significant for the following reasons. First, it involves numerous smallholder farmers, who are expected to collaborate and organise themselves in order to manage water and irrigation. Understanding how farmers are getting on with managing the

---

68   FDRE 2010; 2014
69   Beyene and Sandström 2016; Bues and Theesfeld 2012
70   Oestigaard 2012
71   FDRE 2011
72   The others being protection and rehabilitation of forests for their economic and ecosystem services as carbon stocks; and use of appropriate advanced technologies in industry, transport and buildings.

scheme is crucial. Second, the irrigation scheme induces a radical shift in farming practices – from a predominantly rain-fed to a predominantly irrigated agricultural system. This entails an adjustment in the allocation of household resources for farming. Third, the scheme involves different actors with different stakes. Finally, such initiatives are relatively new to the country. Hence, the lessons have important implications for other similar projects that are under construction.

Type of Works	2010/11	2011/12	2012/13			2014/15
	Actual	Actual	Plan	Actual	Achieved (%)	Target
Irrigation development study and design	178,820	98,055	146,951	263,645	179.4	1,208,448
Irrigation development construction	32,034	42,229	124,624	96,650	77.6	785,583
Rehabilitation and maintenances	-	-	1,000	4,100	410	6,570
Small Sale Irrigation (MoA)	1,064,200	1,460,000	1,660,000	1,830,000	110.2	260,000

Figure 3.4. Performance of medium, large and small scale irrigation from 2010/11 to 2012/13 (in hectares, ha). Source: Ministry of Water, Irrigation and Energy and Ministry of Agriculture (in FDRE 2014, p. 57, table 28).

Irrigation – underdeveloped, but emerging

Ethiopia's economy is mainly dependent on agriculture. Agriculture contributes 40 per cent to GDP and employs 80 per cent of the population.[73] The two dominant agricultural systems are the mixed farming and the pastoral systems. The mixed farming system, where farmers combine both crop and livestock production, is mainly located in the highlands, where population density is high and land holdings are very small – about 1 hectare (ha) of land per household.[74] These systems are predominantly rain-fed, and the dependency on rainfall has been recognised as a major source of vulnerability. Recurrent drought, variability of rainfall and climate change have seriously challenged the agricultural sector. Irrigation has been identified as a means of adapting to and mitigating climate change impacts in the agricultural systems.

Ethiopia's irrigation agriculture is relatively underdeveloped, compared to other African countries. Of the total 12.28 million ha of cultivated land in 2006, only 5 per cent was irrigated.[75] Most of the irrigated area (77 per cent) was under small-scale

---

73   FDRE 2011
74   CSA 2014
75   MoFED 2006

traditional irrigation system.[76] Traditional irrigation schemes have no permanent diversion structures and are reconstructed every year from local materials by the farmers themselves. They constitute free flood-intake, furrow systems and river diversions. More recently spate irrigation, water pumps and small ponds have been reported in different parts of the country.[77]

However, the potential for irrigation is big. Estimates indicate that Ethiopia has 5.3 million ha of land that is suitable for irrigation, of which 3.7 million ha can be developed using surface water sources, and 1.6 million ha using groundwater and rainwater management.[78] In its recent plans, the government spelt out that it intends to expand agricultural production by an additional 3 million ha, with the addition of small- and large-scale irrigation schemes.[79] Over the short term, interventions in small-scale schemes are seen as enabling the country to leverage its abundant labour, while reaching rural households and communities. In this regard, community-based small-scale dam constructions and river diversions are set as targets. As a long-term plan, the expansion of modern, large-scale irrigation schemes is high on the policy agenda.

Policy drive for modern irrigation for smallholders

Not only has 'modern'[80] irrigation a short history in the country, but also it has almost no association with smallholder farmers.[81] Very few modern irrigation systems were introduced in the 1960s and 1970s, and their significance in terms of area coverage has been very low. In 2009, it was reported that Ethiopia's modern irrigation system represented only 1.6 per cent of the total cultivated area.[82] However, this appears to have been changing fast over the past decade, as irrigation schemes expand across the country. Modern irrigation systems are seen as long-term projects with the aim of bringing about economic growth and overcoming the challenge of the correlation between rainfall and agricultural growth.[83] Hence, such initiatives are seen as especially important for the country's development plan.[84]

With four large-scale dams completed and in use for irrigation, four currently under construction and 15 more planned,[85] the area under dammed irrigation will be significant. Some of the dams are multipurpose, covering hydropower, fisheries and irrigation; others are constructed to provide irrigation facilities for small-scale agricul-

---

76 Hagos et al. 2009
77 Belay and Bewket 2013; Steenbergen et al. 2011
78 Awulachew and Ayana 2011
79 Conniff et al. 2012
80 In this sense, engineered and permanent water management systems dedicated to irrigation, with high levels of technology, bureaucracy and material inputs.
81 Rami 2003
82 Hagos et al. 2009
83 MoWR 2006; 2002
84 Awulachew 2010
85 Verhoeven 2011

ture. During the first three years of the GTP period (2010-2013), feasibility studies and design works for large- and medium-scale irrigation schemes were undertaken on a total of 541,000 ha of land.[86] During the same period, construction work on large- and medium-scale irrigation schemes was undertaken on 171,000 ha.[87] By the end of the GTP in 2015, the total land under medium- and large-scale irrigation was expected to have reached 786,000 ha. Notable megaprojects here are the five sugarcane plantations under construction by the Ethiopian Sugar Corporation.[88]

The introduction of medium- and large-scale irrigation schemes for smallholder farmers is also a major part of the modernisation process covered by the current policies. Although the large-scale irrigation schemes continue to be largely under public management, recently there have been efforts by the government to involve smallholders in the use and management of modern schemes. The promise of this approach is that – by improving the storage of water and its availability for irrigation by smallholder farmers – dams and irrigation schemes will create employment and improve food security among smallholder farmers in rural areas. The flip side of this is that the changes and adaptations that the smallholders must make in order to operationalise the planned irrigation schemes are enormous. The shift from predominantly rain-fed to predominantly irrigation agriculture entails changes in farming practices. Above all, the new production schemes require collective action and coordination of management among water users and stakeholders. Changes are also required in policies and the institutional framework, in order to support smallholders' use and management of the new irrigation production system.

Collective management and collaboration

In his book entitled *Seeing Like a State*, political scientist and anthropologist James C. Scott asks why certain schemes that are intended to improve the human condition fail.[89] Large-scale irrigation schemes often face critical sustainability challenges in many parts of the world.[90] A common feature is that while governments are often swift to construct and deliver physical aspects of irrigation infrastructures, the establishment of governance systems that can support sustainable use and management of such infrastructure is challenging.

The case study scheme involves not only numerous water-user households, but also different stakeholders. Central in this regard is coordination of the management of the scheme. The alternatives in this are central or decentralised management, or a combination of both. Some argue that for large-scale irrigation schemes, central administration is more effective. Formal monitoring and administration of irrigation schemes

---

86   FDRE 2014
87   ibid.
88   Ethiopian Sugar Corporation http://ethiopiansugar.com/index.php/en/ (accessed 9 December 2017).
89   Scott 1998
90   Callejo and Cossio 2009; Garces-Restrepo et al. 2007

might be effective in implementing projects, but may not guarantee sustainability and efficiency.[91] Others indicate that decentralised management of irrigation is better.[92] Related to this is the self-organised management of irrigation schemes as an important condition for the development of a sustainable management structure.[93]

This chapter presents a case study, where management of the scheme combines elements of both central and decentralised systems. To explore the social and institutional aspects of irrigation management, this chapter explores practices involving the physical maintenance of the canal systems, financial recovery mechanisms, distribution of water and watershed management.

Case Study: Koga Dam and Irrigation Scheme

Physical infrastructure and scheme layout

The Koga Dam and Irrigation Scheme is a large-scale dam and irrigation scheme in the Lake Tana Basin in northwestern Ethiopia. Construction has been completed and irrigation has started. Therefore, it provides an interesting opportunity to study the prospects and challenges so far, as well as to draw lessons that may be directly relevant for the other projects under construction. The scheme was constructed in 2008 by the Ethiopian Ministry of Water and Energy at an initial cost of USD 50 million, to provide irrigation for small-scale agriculture. Irrigation agriculture started in 2010.

According to the International Commission on Large Dams classification criteria,[94] the Koga Dam can be classified as a large dam. The infrastructure includes the dam (reserve capacity of 81.3 million cubic metres) and 12 water storage and command facilities located along an almost 20 km main canal. There is also a 42.4 km secondary canal, 112 km of lined and unlined tertiary canals, 97 km of drainage canals and 2,921 concrete and masonry structures. The dam can irrigate about 7,000 ha and can benefit about 14,000 smallholder farm households. According to the project plan, the irrigation scheme should lead to an additional production of 15,000 tonnes of maize, 24,000 tonnes of potatoes, 18,000 tonnes of onions and 5,400 tonnes of wheat.[95] In March 2014, 5,800 ha were put under cultivation by a total of about 7,300 farm

---

91 Hunt 1988
92 Carlsson and Berkes 2005
93 Ostrom 1990
94 A large dam is defined as any dam above 15 metres in height (measured from the lowest point of foundation to the top of the dam) or any dam between 10 and 15 metres in height which meets at least one of the following conditions: a) the crest length is not less than 500 metres; b) the capacity of the reservoir formed by the dam is not less than 1 million cubic metres; c) the maximum flood discharge dealt with by the dam is not less than 2,000 cubic metres per second; d) the dam had especially difficult foundation problems; e) the dam is of unusual design. Source: http://www.icold-cigb.net/ (accessed 9 December 2017).
95 AfDB 2001

Facts about the Koga dam and its irrigation scheme
Source: Abbay Basin Authority Koka Water Structure Management and Water Administration Centre, Chaha Woreda Office.

- Catchment area 22,000 hectares
- Dam height 21.5 m
- Dam crest length 1,730 m
- Reservoir area 1,750 hectares
- Dam water holding capacity 81.3 million m³
- Main canal discharge 9.1 m³/sec
- 19.7 km main canal

- 12 water storage and command facilities (located along the main canal)
- 112 km lined and unlined tertiary canals
- Number of beneficiary family heads 14,000
- Total irrigation land 7,002 hectares
- Irrigated land (March 2014) 5,828 hectares

Figure 3.5. Water transmission pipe supplying Addis Ababa, at a distance of more than 500 km from Koga, with potable water.

households.[96] The Koga Dam has a catchment of 22,000 ha. Watershed management programmes (including soil and water conservation and forestry programmes to reduce soil loss by 50 per cent) are part of the project plan.[97]

The irrigation area is divided into 12 blocks, with an average size of 583 ha (minimum 290 ha and maximum 864 ha). Each block has its own water storage area, which is an excavated large open pond, where the pond bottom is reinforced with fine soil materials, plastic sheets and some concrete materials. These ponds are distributed along the roughly 20 km main canal at suitable locations, so that gravity irrigation is possible. A network of secondary canals leads the water over the block areas. The tertiary canal networks then lead the water to each farm boundary. Each farmer then applies furrow irrigation to his or her plot. The furrows are parallel ditches constructed on the field by the farmers using animal traction or by hand.

---

96 Beyene, unpublished field report
97 AfDB 2001

Command and water storage area	Irrigated area (ha)	Length of secondary canals (metres)	Length of lined tertiary canals (metres)	Length of tertiary un-lined canals (metres)	Length of drains (metres)	Concrete structures (number)	Benefici-ary households (number)
Kudmi	373	875	1,901	6,838	4,582	238	746
Chihona	617	3756	1,389	9,412	6,307	240	1,234
Inguti	393	779	3,599	3,670	5,540	218	786
Ambo Mesk	812	7,186	1,855	10,550	10,312	251	1,624
Adbera Mariam	803	8,054	695	11,659	4,408	314	1,606
Lasi	484	2,505	1,601	7,321	6,970	176	968
Bered	468	2,875	3,523	4,501	6,282	189	936
Andnet	497	2,641	1,852	4,378	7,891	163	994
Amarit	290	868	392	5,207	4,419	106	580
Tegel Wedefit	616	4,472	1,850	6,810	9,655	322	1,232
Tekel Dib	864	5,530	5,810	6,256	18,857	340	1,728
Telata	787	2,841	4,233	6,822	11,926	271	1,574
TOTAL	**7,004**	**42,382**	**28,700**	**83,424**	**97,149**	**2,828**	**14,008**

Figure 3.6. Irrigation command areas, canals and beneficiaries of the Koga Irrigation Scheme. Source: Abbay Basin Authority Koka Water Structure Management and Water Administration Centre, Chaha Woreda.

Focus on food security and smallholder farmers

Interestingly, the primary purpose of the irrigation project is to provide access to irrigation for smallholder farmers in the local areas. Access to adequate water, agricultural inputs and agricultural services, such as extension services, forms part of the projects. The ambition of this project is to move the smallholder farming system from the current subsistence practices towards more productive and commercially oriented practices. Improving livelihoods, food security and rural employment are key objectives of the project. Other economic objectives include expansion of private commercial farms, fishery and tourism.

Farmer displacement, compensation and land consolidation

The dam and irrigation project involved programmes of displacement of farmers from the water dam site. In this process, the farmers were compensated for the properties they lost. Cash was paid for lost properties, such as houses, farms and other long-term investments, (such as trees and conservation structures). This programme was assisted financially by the World Bank. In addition to the cash, the farmers were given a plot of land to build their houses and irrigation land from the irrigation project.

Major farm consolidation and redistribution programmes were also carried out in 2009 to pave the way for the irrigation schemes. This involved all farms located in the irrigable area. Previously, household farms used to be fragmented and located in different areas. With the land consolidation programme, all farms that fell within the irrigable downstream area were put together (consolidated) and a new redistribution was carried out among the households. The households were given 80 per cent of their respective previous landholdings. The 20 per cent deducted from each farm household downstream was transferred to the government for various purposes, but mainly to accommodate farmers who lost land because of the dam water body and to create a land reserve for private investors.

Stakeholders and canal management setup

The key stakeholders involved in the project are the Ethiopian government, the World Bank, the African Development Bank and the rural people. The role of the banks has been limited to financial support for the construction of the project and the compensation of displaced farmers. They were also involved in impact assessment and appraisal studies of the project. The government has been the major actor in key areas such as financing, construction, distribution of land and water, and the organisation of local people. These activities involved a number of government agencies. While the construction of the project was undertaken by the Ministry of Water and Energy, the Abbay Basin Authority Agency was tasked with regulating the distribution of water at the main outlets. It has a mandate to administer the dam, as well as the primary and secondary canals. The mandate includes regulating the release of water at the main dam outlet, the refilling and release of water at the 12 water storage sites, as well as the release of water at secondary canals. To administer these, experts from the basin authority are stationed in the local area.

The Ministry of Agriculture and Rural Development is involved in introducing extension services on irrigation and in providing agricultural inputs, such as improved seeds and fertiliser for the farmers. Land allocation, registration and certification are managed by the Rural Land Administration Bureau.

The government, through the Cooperative Promotion Agency (CPA), has also organised the households into 12 water 'cooperative' groups. In principle, the farmers in each block are aggregated into a water 'cooperative' group. These groups are irrigation beneficiaries and are responsible for managing the tertiary canals.

The water 'cooperatives' were more or less created by the CPA. The agency applies a general policy directive that was developed for cooperatives. Since the shift of government in 1991, there have been renewed efforts to revitalise policies on cooperatives. A legislative framework on the promotion and establishment of cooperatives came into force in 1994.[98] In 1998 and 2004, there were additional proclamations that reinforce the principles and strengthen membership incentives by improving members' rights in the areas of ownership, voting, share transfer and risk management.[99] The CPA (under the Ministry of Trade) facilitates the formation of cooperatives. It has offices at the federal, regional zonal and district levels of government.

---

98   Proclamation 85/1994.
99   Proclamations 147/1998 and 402/2004.

Irrigation cooperatives, which in 2009 constituted less than 4 per cent of cooperatives,[100] are one of the many types of cooperatives established by the CPA. The practice in general is quite similar, as they follow the general rules and directives, and the CPA at the local level is involved in initiating and/or facilitating the process (figure 3.7 indicates provision at the local level).

THE COOPERATIVE PROMOTION AGENCY is tasked with organising farmers into cooperatives in various economic sectors, of which irrigation is one. The agency has developed models on the formation and internal regulations of the cooperatives. For the irrigation cooperatives, the model constitutes the following aspects.

PART I – GENERAL: It offers legal frameworks for the recognition of cooperative entities. It identifies the cooperative by specific name, date of establishment, number of members and definition and clarification of terms (such as irrigation and watershed).

PART II – ADMINISTRATION: Cooperatives, through their elected committees, are responsible for the protection and management of irrigation facilities. The committees are responsible for compiling data (on land to be irrigated, types of crops to be planted, and number of beneficiaries for each season) and communicating this to the bureau of agriculture one month in advance of the start of the cropping time. Irrigation and agronomic decisions are then approved at an assembly meeting that involves all beneficiaries.

Users that are not members of the cooperatives must ensure a contractual agreement with the water cooperatives in order to get access to irrigation water.

PART III – CANAL DEVELOPMENT PRACTICES: Through the general assembly, establishment of an executive committee, a control committee and a management and administration committee that oversee the cooperative's canal development activities.

Figure 3.7. Irrigation Cooperative Internal Model Regulations, Cooperative Promotion Agency, Amhara Regional State, 2011, Bahir Dar.

Issues and gaps in irrigation management

A major implication of the above processes is that there is a lot of restructuring and a tremendous drive by the state and other agencies to promote irrigation among smallholder farmers. The broader policy agenda to promote agriculture and develop the infrastructure seems to have paved the way for a centralised and interventionist approach to restructuring. Interviews with local officials from the various bureaus and authorities, as well as with farmers, indicate a number of issues and gaps in management of the irrigation systems.

---

100 Emana 2009

Challenges in coordination

Poor coordination was indicated by local officials as one of the major challenges in the management of the scheme. This challenge was particularly emphasised with regard to government agencies. As an example, coordination challenges between the Koga Basin Authority (KBA) and the Ministry of Agriculture and Rural Development (MARD) were indicated as undermining the plan and the forecasting of water requirements. While the KBA is responsible for documentation, for forecasting, budgeting and distributing water over the whole scheme, the MARD is responsible for the crop and agronomic support system of the irrigation scheme. Both agencies have offices at the Woreda administrative level. The main problem indicated was that the planning for the water budget and water allocation did not take account of the type and coverage of crops: information on crop types, area to be covered, frequency of cropping by farmers, etc. was not provided by the MARD to the KBA in good time, before the cropping season started. This poses challenges to farmers who plan to have two harvests during the dry season.

To address this, a knowledge-exchange system that allows stakeholders to share information and responsibility is necessary.

Uncertainty and poor sense of ownership in the early stages of the project

According to the informants, resistance from, and uncertainty among, local farmers were both high when the project was initiated. One of the reasons for this was that introduction of the scheme was going to reduce the population of their livestock, as the seasonal grazing area was allocated to the permanent irrigation area, from which the livestock would be permanently excluded. Today, the free grazing area is too limited to maintain the previous livestock population. Instead, cut-and-carry feeding systems are used, and the animals are kept in the household compounds. This has reduced both the number of households that keep livestock and the livestock population.

Another reason indicated for farmer resistance was that the irrigated area disrupted communication between villages. Because the area put under irrigation is big and roads across the fields were not included in the construction design, it is not easy to reach villages on the other side of the irrigation area. According to the farmers, this was one reason why they resisted the project, at least in its initial stages.

The farmers' lack of a sense of ownership of the canals was also indicated by the local agricultural extension workers as a challenge in managing the irrigation scheme. Damage to canals and canal banks – for example, siltation and the accumulation of debris along the secondary and tertiary canals – sometimes caused water to overflow into adjacent fields, and this was frequently cited as a problem. Damage to the canals caused by livestock was also highlighted as a problem. While all this may indicate a poor sense of ownership, the underlying reasons need to be explored further.

Maintenance of the tertiary and drainage canals

The total length of the tertiary canals, both lined and unlined, is 112 km, and there are 97 km of drainage canals (see figure 3.6). This indicates a high density of canals in the irrigation area. Furthermore, individual farmers own and cultivate on average less than 1 ha. This all makes it highly complex business, and the internal systems of water flows can easily be disrupted if an individual farmer fails to look after the canals on his farm boundary. The general practice is that each farmer is responsible for clearing the canal of weeds and soil deposits and for maintaining the canal banks adjacent to his plot boundaries. Farmers mentioned that the banks can easily shift during the cropping season, leading to situations where either the water does not flow properly to the next user or there is excess application in particular areas.

According to those farmers interviewed, farmers who lease irrigation plots over a cropping season often do not care much when it comes to maintaining canal banks. Other reasons mentioned include instability of the banks and shortage of land (leading some farmers to chip away at canal banks and boundaries to expand their area). Monitoring and supervision of these processes is often difficult, as they take place at the micro-level.

Non-uniformity in cropping and water demands

Farmers use surface flooding to irrigate their plots. This method of irrigation is wasteful. Farmers in general lack the means to know and evaluate their current on-farm water-efficiency levels. Furthermore, differences in farmer capacities were indicated as a source of inequality in water use. Depending on their capacity, farmers may choose different crops to plant, and the crops may have different levels of water demands; this complicates the relationships between farmers. As the farmers interviewed indicated, some of them manage to harvest twice during the dry season, while others are able to produce only once. Those who harvest twice often plant fast-growing crops, such as vegetables, which normally have high water demand. These farmers were generally described as well-off farmers who have the resources.

The leasing of plots, which is practised among the farmers themselves, was also indicated as a reason for the differences in water use. Those who lease out their land were described as relatively poor or mainly female-headed households. The tenants, may be relatively better-off farmers or landless young people who have earned cash through off-farm or non-farming activities. In order to pay the cost of the lease and to maximise their returns, these farmers were reported to be generally efficient and their water requirement relatively high. These everyday local-level differences in production capacities entail questions of equitable distribution of irrigation water.

The question of protecting the catchment area of the dam

The dam catchment area is about 22,000 ha. Although the number of people living in the catchment was not ascertained from the local office, some farmers do live and cultivate in the catchment area. Except for those living at the dam site, none of the farmers in the catchment area were displaced. According to the project plan, conservation activities are supposed to be carried out in the catchment area to reduce siltation. As an expert at the Bureau of Agriculture indicated, the dilemma was that the farmers in the catchment area, who were supposed to practise conservation agriculture and approve the closure of the area for rehabilitation of degraded and vulnerable land, did not benefit from the scheme. This has created a rift between the upstream and downstream farmers.

Market outputs and post-harvest challenges

The current focus of the irrigation scheme is overwhelmingly on improving access to agricultural inputs. These include water, seeds, fertilisers and extension services. However, initiatives to address output market linkages are sadly lacking. This gap has created insecurity among farmers when it comes to marketing their products at a reasonable profit. 'Dumping' especially of perishable products, such as potatoes, which are also bulky, was indicated as a major obstacle. According to informants, a kilo of potatoes was being sold for 1 Ethiopian Birr (equivalent to 3 US cents) in the 2012/13 harvesting season. Shortcomings in transport and storage facilities were other important factors limiting the potential of farmers to uncover better market alternatives.

Related to the market output challenge is the whole chain of post-harvest losses of crops, including harvesting and drying, threshing, transport, on-farm storage and transport to market.[101] Poor post-harvest management in general is a common problem across resource-poor smallholders in Africa, leading to loss of 20-30 per cent, with an estimated monetary value of more than USD 4 billion annually.[102] Studies on post-harvest losses in the major cereal crops produced by smallholder farmers in Ethiopia indicate a similar percentage of crop losses.[103]

Conclusions

This exploratory study addresses the main features and processes involved in irrigation schemes, and some challenges facing their management. The case study presented offers a context where the mainstream development policy is central not only to creating the physical structures (schemes), but also to creating the organisational and institutional set-up to run the schemes. The notion of creating new institutions and organisations, adapting them to the physical and social realities and extending the realm of governance from the domains of formalised decision making in water allocation into everyday interactions by the local people brings with it an array of issues. These include the role of the state, power inequalities and control over resources. For instance, the political discourse on the need to expand the irrigation infrastructure reinforces the role of the

---

101 Tefera 2012
102 FAO 2010
103 Hodges et al. 2011

state. One effect of this is that state agencies are heavily engaged in water allocation and distribution. This engagement has become important in water decision-making processes at the scheme level.

The irrigation system involves a plurality of arrangements. Hence, far from being simply a site to access water, the scheme needs to be seen as a site of multiple objectives. While some agencies are tasked with developing the infrastructure, others are responsible for the distribution of water resources. Other actors – such as the Bureau of Agriculture – are involved in promoting new agricultural practices and inputs. In this process, farmers are increasingly drawn into the objectives and arrangements of those powerful actors. A clear trend noted in this study is that farmers become increasingly dependent on state agencies. For instance, the administration and distribution of water across the whole scheme is performed by the agencies.

Another overarching question is whether formalised and bureaucratic approaches to irrigation management guarantee sustainable use of the resources. The creation and registration of cooperatives, land consolidation and redistribution are all part of the top-down formalisation process. These measures can be seen as crucial steps in making sure that the planned irrigation project become operational. However, there are limitations to this approach – not least the fact that it does not recognise the local actions of the water users. Everyday activities related to water use, maintenance of canal systems, differences in water demands, etc. were reported by water users as important. Understanding the informal negotiation and everyday creativity are at least equally important in reproducing the institutional and organisational arrangements that are neither entirely customary nor wholly bureaucratic, but something new and different.

To summarise, the major paradox in management is that, while the role of the state in the management of irrigation infrastructure continues to be strong and indispensable, there is a realisation that canal and water management should be transferred to the users, in order to reduce the cost of operation and maintenance. Promoting user participation and self-management to ensure good institutional and organisational arrangements that are responsible for the operation and maintenance of the infrastructure, water access and distribution, as well as for financial sustainability for the current and future operational costs, is perhaps the priority issue that needs to be addressed.

References

AfDB (African Development Bank) (2001), Koga Irrigation and Watershed Management Project: Appraisal report. Abidjan.

Awulachew, S. (2010), Irrigation Potential in Ethiopia: Constraints and opportunities for enhancing the system. International Water Management Institute,.

Awulachew, S. and M. Ayana (2011), Performance of irrigation: An assessment at different scales in Ethiopia, Experimental Agriculture, 47: 57-69.

Belay, M. and W. Bewket (2013), Traditional irrigation and water management practices in highland Ethiopia. Case study in Dangila Woreda, Irrigation and Drainage, 62: 435-448.

Beyene, A. and E. Sandström (2016), Emerging water frontiers in large-scale land acquisitions and implications for food security in Africa. In: T. Tvedt and T. Oestigaard (eds), A History of Water: Water and food in Africa. London: IB Tauris, pp. 502-520.

Bues, A. and I. Theesfeld (2012), Water grabbing and the role of power: Shifting water governance in the light of agricultural foreign direct investment, Water Alternatives, 5/2: 266-283.

Callejo, I. and I. Cossio (2009), Institutional aspects of sustainability for irrigated agriculture in arid and semi-arid regions, Chilean Journal of Agricultural Research, 69 (Suppl. 1): 41-53.

Carlsson, L. and F. Berkes (2005), Co-management: Concepts and methodological implications, Journal of Environmental Management, 75/1: 65-76.

Conniff, K., D. Molden, D. Peden and S. Awulachew (2012), Nile water and agriculture: Past, present and future. In: S. Awulachew, V. Smakhtin, D. Molden and D. Peden (eds), The Nile River Basin: Water, agriculture, governance. Routledge, London.

CSA (Central Statistical Agency) (2014), Land Utilization: Private peasant holdings, meher season. Agricultural Sample Survey 2014/2015, Vol. IV. Central Statistical Agency of Ethiopia, Addis Ababa.

Emana, B. (2009), Cooperatives: A path to economic and social empowerment in Ethiopia, CoopAFRICA Working Paper No. 9. International Labour Organization, Dar es Salaam.

FAO (Food and Agriculture Organization) (2010), Reducing post-harvest losses in grain supply chains in Africa: Lessons learned and practical guidelines. FAO/World Bank Workshop 18-19 March. FAO Headquarters, Rome.

FDRE (Federal Democratic Republic of Ethiopia) (2010), Growth and Transformation Plan 2010/11-2014/15. Ministry of Finance and Economic Development (MoFED), Addis Ababa.

FDRE (Federal Democratic Republic of Ethiopia) (2011), Ethiopia's Climate-Resilient Green Economy Strategy: The path to sustainable development. Environmental Protection Authority, Addis Ababa.

FDRE (Federal Democratic Republic of Ethiopia) (2013), Environmental and Social Management Framework (Draft Document), Water Supply and Sanitation Program – WaSh-II, Oct. 2013. Addis Ababa.

FDRE (Federal Democratic Republic of Ethiopia) (2014), Growth and Transformation Plan: Annual Progress Report for Fiscal Year 2012/13. Ministry of Finance and Economic Development, Addis Ababa.

Garces-Restrepo, C., D. Vermillion and G. Munoz (2007), Irrigation Management Transfer: Worldwide efforts and results. Food and Agriculture Organization, Rome.

Gebregziabher, G. (2009), Poverty reduction with irrigation investment: An empirical case study from Tigray, Ethiopia, Agricultural Water Management, 96: 1837-1843.

Hagos, F., G. Makombe, R.E. Namara and S.B. Awulachew (2009), Importance of Irrigated Agriculture to the Ethiopian Economy: Capturing the direct net benefits of irrigation. IWMI Research Report No. 128. International Water Management Institute, Colombo, Sri Lanka.

Hodges, R., J. Buzby and B. Bennett (2011), Postharvest losses and waste in developed and less developed countries: Opportunities to improve resource use, Journal of Agricultural Science, 149: 37-45.

Hunt, R. (1988), Size and the structure of authority in canal irrigation systems, Journal of Anthropological Research, 44/4: 335-355.

MoFED (Ministry of Finance and Economic Development), Ethiopia (2006), A Plan for Accelerated and Sustained Development to End Poverty. Addis Ababa.

MoWR (Ministry of Water Resources), Ethiopia (2002), Water Sector Development Programme 2002–2016. Irrigation Development Program, Main report. Addis Ababa.

MoWR (Ministry of Water Resources), Ethiopia (2006), Five Year Irrigation Development Programme (2005/06–2009/10). Addis Ababa.

Oestigaard, T. (2012), Water scarcity and food security along the Nile: Politics, population increase and climate change, Current African Issues, No. 49. Nordic Africa Institute, Uppsala.

Ostrom, E. (1990), Governing the Commons. Cambridge University Press, New York.

Rami, H. (2003), Ponds Filled with Challenges: Water harvesting – experiences in Amhara and Tigray. Assessment report. UN OCH, Ethiopia.

Scott, J. (1998), Seeing Like a State: How certain schemes to improve the human condition have failed. Yale University Press, New Haven and London.

Steenbergen, F., A. Haile, T. Alemehayu, T. Almirew and Y. Geleta (2011), Status and potential of spate irrigation in Ethiopia, Spate Irrigation Network, January, No. 4.

Tefera, T. (2012), Post-harvest losses in African maize in the face of increasing food shortage, Food Science, 4: 267-277.

Verhoeven, H. (2011), Black Gold for Blue Gold? Sudan's oil, Ethiopia's water and regional integration. Briefing Paper. Chatham House, London.

BUJAGALI FALLS
DANGER
DO NOT GO
BEYOND THIS POINT
MANAGEMENT

If the World Bank had properly understood the complicated processes at work at Bujagali Falls, it might have refused to support the dam.

/ Terje Oestigaard, p. 76

Bujagali Falls, May 2009. Photo: Annette Bouvain, Flickr.

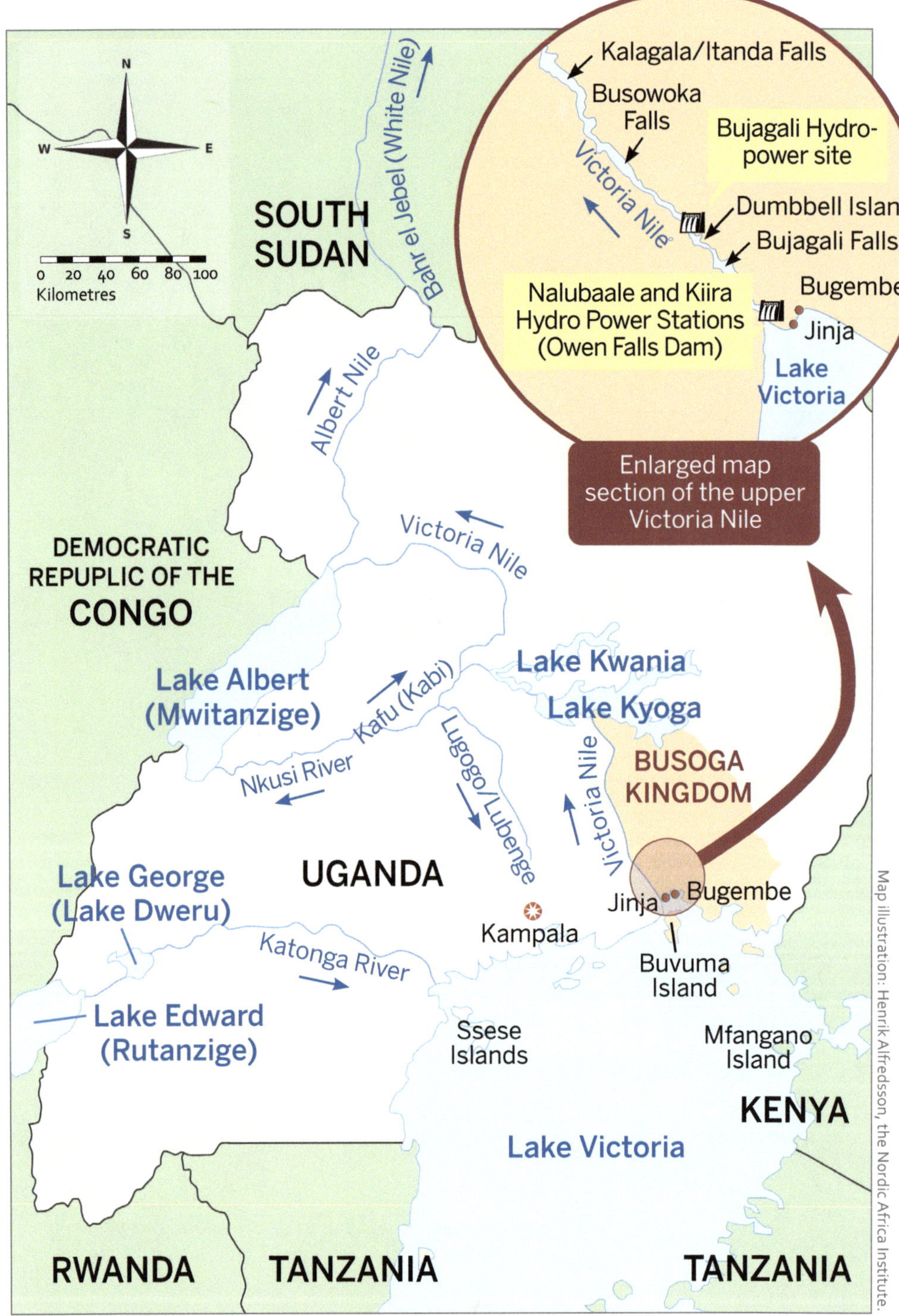

Figure 4.1. Map of Uganda and localisation of the Bujagali Hydro-Power Dam.

CHAPTER 4 [104]

A billion-dollar ritual: Spirit appeasement ceremonies behind the Bujagali Dam

Terje Oestigaard

The Bujagali Hydropower Project in Uganda has been one of the most controversial dam projects of modern times. Located some 8 kilometres north of Jinja and the outlet of Lake Victoria, traditionally regarded as the source of the White Nile, it was Uganda's largest dam when it was inaugurated in 2012. Apart from the general criticism of dams, the Bujagali project has been unique, in the sense that the controversies surrounding it relate to the major water spirit in the culture of the Busoga Kingdom, whose home was to be flooded. In fact, construction of the dam was postponed for years because of this spirit and the fierce disputes between two healers who claimed to be the water spirit's representatives.

Water powers take many forms, and in the Bujagali Falls one may see how technology and cosmology are interlinked in local and global discourse. This analysis places the Bujagali project in context. Why has it been seen as so controversial? What was the ritual drama behind the scenes, when three major appeasement ceremonies were conducted to secure the Budhagaali spirit's blessing for the dam? Why did the healer Nfuudu conduct these rituals, rather than Jaja Bujagali, the healer who embodies the Budhagaali spirit? How did the dam affect the main river spirit and indigenous religion, and is it possible to drown a river spirit in its own element – water? All these questions relate to modernity and development discourses. But with regard to Bujagali, there was one additional factor: how do you negotiate with a spirit?

Bujagali hydropower plant

The Bujagali hydropower plant is situated some 8 kilometres from the Nalubaale and Kiira hydropower plants. The project includes 100 kilometres of transmission lines. There were two phases to the project. The first phase was terminated and the company involved, AES Corporation, pulled out in September 2003, partly because of a corrup-

---

104 This chapter is based on Oestigaard (2015).

tion scandal. At first glance, it is difficult to see why this dam should have been one of the most controversial in recent history, given that the area flooded and the number of people resettled and compensated was relatively small – and indeed much smaller than in most dam projects. The bid for the project in 2000 was USD 447 million.[105] In 2012, the final price tag was estimated to be USD 902 million.[106] Thus by 2012, the price had more than doubled from the initial projected cost.

The Bujagali Hydropower Project involves a 250 MW hydropower facility, comprising a 28-metre-high earth-filled dam and an associated power station with five 50 MW turbines. The reservoir extends upstream to the tail areas of the Nalubaale and Kiira dams (see map, figure 4.1). When full, the reservoir will have a water volume of 54 million cubic metres.[107] In the social and environmental report produced by the construction company, Bujagali Energy Limited, it is noted that 'the reservoir will be 388 ha in surface area [3.9 square kilometres], comprised of the existing 308 ha of the surface of the Victoria Nile, and 80 ha of newly inundated land. The amount of newly inundated land is small, as the reservoir will be contained within the steeply incised banks of the river.' The same report also refers to 88 hectares of inundated land.[108]

When the first stage of the project was terminated, about 8,700 people (1,288 households) had been either moved or compensated. Most of those affected were compensated, and only 634 people (85 households) actually had to move. In some reports there were slightly different numbers: 101 households (714 persons) were physically displaced, while the remaining 1,187 non-physically displaced households were compensated for the loss of crops, trees, land and other assets.[109] Thus, the impact of the dam was slight by any standards of dam construction. Since the reservoir is located in a gorge, only 80-90 hectares of new land were flooded. If the size and impact of the Bujagali Dam are less than is generally the case with dams, why has it been so controversial? The answer is to be found not in Uganda, but in Washington and at the World Commission on Dams (WCD) in Berkeley, California, which launched its report *Dams and Development: A new framework for decision-making* in 2000. The Bujagali Dam became one of the first test cases to see if the World Bank would follow these new guidelines, which effectively would have put an end to all large dam construction worldwide.

Inspection panel and water cosmology

One of the main reasons for the opposition to the Bujagali Dam was what anti-dam campaigners saw as a gap between the decision-making process and the WCD report as the framework for best practices.[110] Frank Muramuzi, from the National Association of

---

105 EIB-CM (2012), p. 28.
106 ERA (2012), p. 16.
107 WB IP (2008), p. 29.
108 Burnside (2006), pp. 1, 27.
109 IDA (2008), p. 25.
110 Conca (2006), p. 208.

Professional Environmentalists, said: 'Constitutionally the project violates environmental protection rights… We will sue government, World Bank or both.'[111] In 2003, F.C. Oweyegha-Afunaduula wrote a short article entitled 'Huge dams as corporate crime and terrorism.'[112] Deputy coordinator of the Save Bujagali Crusade, Oweyegha-Afunaduula was quoted in the Ugandan newspaper *The Voice* (10 May 1999) as saying:

> Bujagali Falls is a cultural, social, ecological, ethical, moral, spiritual and environmental stabiliser for the Busoga, which if implemented would lead to both ethnic cleansing and cultural death of 2.5 million people. Save Bujagali Crusade cannot allow this to happen.[113]

These allegations were repeated in 2004:

> Recent reflections at Save Bujagali Crusade (SBC) and the National Association of Professional Environmentalists (NAPE) on the decision of the Uganda Government to embrace corporate advice to destroy Bujagali Falls for hydropower have taken seriously the coming assault on the 2.5 million Busoga through the violence, ecoterrorism, ethnic-cleansing and human rights eroding capacity of the Bujagali dam. The view of SBC and NAPE is that Bujagali Falls threatens the cultural, spiritual and ethno-survival of the Busoga.[114]

Despite the repeated claims in the media by non-governmental organisations (NGOs) and activists about the importance of the cultural and religious heritage of Bujagali, documentation by them of these fundamental cultural and religious practices is strikingly absent. Conversely, while the World Bank is not generally renowned for its cultural and religious studies (including in relation to water), as regards the Busoga, it undertook a very thorough study. The bank's inspection panel is an independent accountability body within the bank. Those who believe they are adversely affected by a bank project, or who believe that fundamental principles have been violated, can file complaints with it. The inspection panel sums up the main elements of Busoga cosmology thus:

> a) the spirits are innumerable, powerful and frequently cross over into the world of the living and may do both good and bad, b) they inhabit the same world as the living and are associated with animate and inanimate objects throughout the landscape, c) they can move freely without the need of human permission, d) they have differential power, influence, and interest, e) they are hierarchical, somewhat comparable to the Greek Pantheon, f) they influence the health, well-being and the livelihood of the living, g) more powerful spirits communicate through mediums who do not view themselves as capable of negotiating or predicting spirit behavior – they are mediums of the spirit who possesses them, and h) the mediums are selected by the spirits, not by the cultural (political) leaders.[115]

---

111 Oweyegha-Afunaduula and Isaac (2004).
112 Oweyegha-Afunaduula (2003), 2/4: 21.
113 Oweyegha-Afunaduula and Isaac (2004).
114 Oweyegha-Afunaduula and Isaac (2004).
115 WB IP (2008): 169.

Figure 4.2. Jaja Bujagali conducting rituals by the falls. From Jaja Bujagali's private collection and photo album. Photo of the original by Terje Oestigaard. Courtesy: Jaja Bujagali.

All the parties – the government, World Bank, construction team, national and international activists, Busoga people, displaced residents, and healers themselves – agreed from the outset of the project that Bujagali Falls is home to a number of spirits ranging from ancestral and family spirits to one of Busoga's most venerated and powerful spirits, the princely Nabamba Budhagaali. In 2001, the panel noted that the leader of the Ntembe clan was Ntembe Waguma and the diviner (*muswezi*) was Nfuudu. A map made in 2001 showed that there were 16 islands, 32 shrines, 10 large trees, 6 rocks, 20 burial grounds, 2 fireplaces and a forest of particular cultural importance in the immediate project area.[116] These cultural sites were to be flooded.

The cultural strategy of the first phase of the project – a line of practice continued in the second phase – was 'focused on closure, relocating, or appeasing the spirits, compensating when necessary, documenting spiritual appeasement through signed certificates, and setting a finite timeline (originally 6 months in 2001)'.[117]

Appeasement ceremony, 28 September 2001

The management of the dam referred to an 'Agreement for the Mitigation of Cultural Impacts and Appeasement of the *Budhagaali Spirit*', which apparently Na-

---

116 WB IP (2008): 169.
117 WB IP (2008): 186-187.

bamba Budhagaali signed on 21 August 2001. The central aspects of the agreement were:

> For the avoidance of doubt, after providing the agreed facilitation for the appeasement ceremonies, the Company [AES] shall deem and *Nabamba Budhagali* hereby asserts that all requisite cultural ceremonies associated with the interest of *Nabamba Budhagali* within the Project Site have been satisfied, the spirits have been appeased … [the] inundation of the Culture site has been accepted by the spirits … *Nabamba Budhagali* shall have no more claims for re-consulting or re-appeasing the Budhagali spirit.[118]

It is not clear whether it was Jaja Bujagali or Nfuudu who signed this. In any event, this was only one of many agreements and certificates to be signed in the coming years. Moreover, it also represents one of the many misconceptions during the whole process, since a healer cannot sign an agreement that a spirit will never change its mind.

There was one major ceremony conducted to appease the main spirits, though this seems to have been a charade caught up in fraud and lies. It is worth quoting from the inspection panel report:

> On September 28, 2001 at the only large ceremony conducted to appease *"the Budhagaali community spirit"* an unspecified number of clan spiritual leaders, the *baswzi abadhagaali* and important dignitaries from all over Busoga were transported to the site at the Sponsor's expense. The followers of Budhagaali were concerned with the rumor that the construction of the dam would take place at their sacred site. They were satisfied, however, when it was revealed that the dam would not be constructed at the site but 3 kilometers downstream at Dumbbell Island.[119]

Neither the dam builder nor the NGOs present corrected this misunderstanding that the sacred sites would not be destroyed, and it seems that the truth of the location of the dam was not explicitly divulged. In 2001, the project identified:

> [Benedicto] Lubaale Nfuudu as a diviner (*muswezi*) who asserts that the spirit Lubaale is the father of Nabamba Budhagaali spirit. He conducts occasional ceremonies with *buswezi* at the Bujagali Falls to communicate with Lubaale, one of the highest spirits within Busoga cosmology, but different from the Bujagali spirit.

The inspection panel thus concluded: 'This opens the possibility that Bujagali Falls, as a cultural property may be the site of two high spirits of the Busoga, not one.'[120] Moreover, the references to undifferentiated 'Bujagali spirits' makes 'it difficult to determine whether or not there are rival claims or just a rivalry between two spiritual mediums.'[121]

---

118 IDA (2008), p. 22.
119 WB IP (2008): 176.
120 WB IP (2008): 179.
121 WB IP (2008): 177.

Following the 28 September 2001 ceremony financed by the sponsor to relocate the Bujagali spirits, the builders claimed that all three mediums involved had agreed that the compensation had been adequate and that construction could proceed. They prepared a certificate of appeasement for signing, but at a 2 October meeting Jaja Bujagali withheld his endorsement.[122] According to Jaja Bujagali and Busoga spiritual logic, 'he could not sign the document for the Spirit. He also claimed that the ceremony on September 28, 2001, had been called not to conduct the ritual of appeasement but to consult his *buswezi Budhagaali*.'[123] Jaja Bujagali also handed over a memorandum to the World Bank inspection panel officers signed by 75 spiritual mediums and stating that they had never been consulted in the dam process.[124] Moreover, Jaja Bujagali had, from the very beginning, opposed the dam on the grounds that if the spirits were not appeased, they would wreak havoc on the project through construction problems, and would cause death and illness. He concluded: 'The spirits would never allow the dam to be built.'[125]

In early August 2006, the Busoga prime minister expressed concern that the spirits at the falls had not been properly released. At a meeting attended by 9 of the 11 Busoga cultural leaders, all of them reaffirmed that the spirits and the shrines needed to be relocated.[126] The inspection panel found that,

> consistent with Busoga belief, … the spiritual mediums cannot provide assurance as to whether or not the Project could proceed before consulting the Spirits in a manner appropriate to their culture. As Nabamba Bujagali explained … the Spirit speaks through him. Non-believers may view this response as nonsense, believing that spiritual mediums are speaking for themselves. As such, he can provide no guarantee.[127]

The panel also stressed the importance of recognising 'that mediums of the Nabamba Budhagaali derive their power through the recognition by the traditional clan priests (*muswezi*) as agents of their believers. The mediums of the high Busoga spirits are incapable of commanding their followers.'[128] Moreover, the spirits decide for themselves if they want to move, and no ritual, regardless of expense or number of animals sacrificed, could change that. After all, gods are gods, spirits are spirits, and humans are humans, and that is the cosmological order.

In any event, Lubaale Nfuudu felt that the spirits had been temporarily relocated to his place, and would then be relocated again to shrines near the project site (Figure 4.3). Nfuudu argued that the spirit Lubaale, one of the high spirits in Busoga cosmology, is the father of the Nabamba Budhagaali spirit. As such, he conducted several rituals and consultations with Lubaale at Bujagali Falls. Although perceived as a single father, the two spirits are nevertheless distinct.

---

122 WB IP (2008): 178.
123 WB IP (2008): 179.
124 Oweyegha-Afunaduula and Isaac (2004).
125 Lacey (2001).
126 WB IP (2008): 172.
127 WB IP (2008): 180.
128 WB IP (2008): 174.

Figure 4.3. Nfuudu's ritual compound in 2013. Photo: Terje Oestigaard.

Relocation ceremony, 19 August 2007

The relocation ceremony on 19 August 2007 was conducted only two days prior to the official ground breaking for the dam, and as such cleared away the last impediment to the Bujagali Dam. When President Museveni laid the foundation stone at a ceremony on 21 August 2007, he said: 'You cannot claim to be protecting the environment when you are denying over 90 percent of the population access to electricity.' Development and industrialisation were the priorities, not culture and indigenous religion.

A Ugandan newspaper characterised the ritual as 'bizarre': 'The disturbing question was how the spirits could be resettled since they were not like the Internally Displaced People in northern Uganda who at least are given seeds, pangas and hoes to start a new life.' Moreover, 'unusual as it may appear, the Busoga traditional healers bulldozed it [the spirit] and performed rituals at Bujagali in Jinja to relocate spirits from the falls … [However] the spirits had earlier already been "removed" from the falls and kept by Jajja Nfuudu … only waiting to be resettled.'

The developers had bought a new piece of land in accordance with the compensation agreement.

> [T]he healers were called to perform at the exercise and one, Nfuudu was given all the necessary requirements which included, goats, sheep, cowries, clay pots, and beads to appease the gods … Nfuudu was mandated to take measurements for the shrines at the new site with respect to the cultures of the land as recommended

by the Busoga Kingdom … the Kingdom officials prefer working with Nfuudu because the spirits "acknowledged" him.

Still, not all the hereditary chiefs were satisfied with the ritual,

> arguing that the spirits will be missing the chance of "enjoying" the water … they only agreed to relocate the spirits but not the site [suggesting that] the spirits would have been asked to choose a site because the eight kilometres from the falls [to the new shrines] seem like chasing the spirits from the water where they were "created".

The representative of Bujagali Energy Limited (BEL), on the other hand, Dr Florence Nangendo, was satisfied: 'We are here to resettle the spirits so that the dam can go on. The project respects cultural sites and cultural beliefs.'[129]

The transfer of the spirit was symbolic. Nfuudu placed a spear wrapped in bark cloth in the roaring waters of Bujagali Falls, holding the spear there for some time before pulling it out and later taking it to the new site at Namizi West, some 8 kilometres from the Bujagali Falls, where the new shrines were not completed. This was the final relocation of the spirits, the healers agreed. 'The spirits have accepted to relocate. To prove that they were happy, there was rain as we relocated them. This will allow the construction and completion of the Bujagali hydropower project successfully,' said James Christopher Mutyaba, the leader of the healers. The chairman of the Busoga chiefdoms sacrificed three cows, twenty goats and chickens at the three new temporary shrines, which had been hurriedly built of brick. 'The blood sacrifice is to get the spirits embedded under the River Nile waters to relocate. This is a clear testimony that we are behind the project.' For three days the festivities went on:

> they sang, feasted on meat, matooke and drank local brew during the rituals that kicked off on Sunday and ended yesterday. Dressed in bark cloths and beads, joyful elderly men and women numbering about 30, smoked tobacco in long brightly decorated pipes as they danced at their new site worth over sh [Ugandan shillings] 11m. The whole relocation exercise cost about sh 21m. Project developers, Bujagali Energy Limited, purchased the site measuring 1.2 acres, following a compensation agreement.[130]

However, at that time the three new shrines at Namizi were merely temporary structures, and it was said that the spirits could not move to unfinished shrines. The road to the shrines was in bad condition and was impassable during periods of rain, and there was no electricity or water facilities at the shrines. BEL had released 21 million Ugandan shillings for the appeasement and relocation of the spirits, which included buying land for the shrines in the village. Nevertheless, since the shrines were not completed, the money was spent on relocating the spirits to Nfuudu's place. 'Even though the

---

129 Kitimbo (2007).
130 Kitimbo (2007).

Figure 4.4. The Bujagali dam. Photo: Terje Oestigaard.

consumables at the time were not worth what was budgeted for, the fact remains that the food was consumed and a plan needs to be made to address the issue at hand,' said the permanent secretary of the Busoga. As an NGO witness report noted:

> The spirits have not reached their final destination. The shrines have not been completed because funds were not ample ... According to the Busoga Kingdom, several items that were crucial were omitted in the previous budget ... It was resolved that the Kingdom submits another budget to complete the construction of the shrines ... [and] it was also agreed that the Busoga Kingdom presents accountability of previous expenses for construction of the shrines and the relocation ceremonies worth Ug Shs 21 million that was given to the Kingdom by BEL.[131]

Thus, the ritual was worth almost 1 billion dollars, since it paved the way for the dam, which eventually had that price tag. But the cost of the ritual was only 21 million Ugandan shillings, which in 2007 currency was about USD 12,500.

---

131 IAU (2010), pp. 27-28.

Final relocation ceremony, 21 June 2011

There was one last ceremony in this ritual drama. The European Investment Bank also contributed loans to the second phase of the Bujagali Dam. As with the World Bank, the European Investment Bank has an independent complaints mechanism. And as with the World Bank, it was NAPE, together with other organisations, that filed complaints that the bank had violated its own policies and practices. This complaint was submitted on 2 December 2009. According to standard procedure, the European Investment Bank Complaints Mechanism (EIB-CM) evaluated the complaints and published its findings in a separate report.[132] One complaint concerned the 2007 ritual, and correctly argued:

> Cultural and spiritual resettlement: No proper consultation ever took place with Bujagali and the spiritual community of the Bujagali Falls. Instead, Jaja Bujagali was marginalised from the process, and a fake resettlement ceremony was organised with the complicity of the Government of Uganda. As a result, no proper spiritual resettlement ever took place.[133]

The spirit Nabamba Budhagaali and its medium, Jaja Bujagali, 'are unquestionably tied to the 338 Busoga clans', and the spirit can possess a spiritual leader from any of these clans. Moreover, as the EIB-CM emphasised, 'notwithstanding all the items surrounding the spiritual issues it is clear … that Jaja Budhagaali [sic] was recognised before as the rightful spiritual leader and that somehow he needs to be taken into consideration in order to progress … in the best possible way.'[134]

In response to the complaint,

> in January 2011, a tripartite "Agreement for the Final Relocation and Appeasement of the Bujagali Spirits" was signed between the Busoga Kingdom, the Government of Uganda and BEL. This agreement defines the role and responsibilities of the … parties involved in terms of the (i) construction of shrines and (ii) organisation of the appeasement ceremonies and ensures the involvement of all key spiritual mediums, including Jaja Budhagaali [sic] and Lubaale Nfuudu. The agreement also accounts for undertakings to avoid any future claims regarding spirits relocation and appeasement.[135]

In a letter of 11 February 2010, the prime minister of the Busoga kingdom stated that Lubaale Nfuudu was the recognised spiritual medium of the kingdom, and declared that the Busoga kingdom 'shall accommodate Nabamba Budhagali [sic] and make him accept the status quo.'[136]

Not surprisingly, although it was acknowledged that Jaja Bujagali had been bypassed and although NAPE characterised the 2007 ritual as fake, the intention of bringing

---

132 EIB-CM (2012).
133 EIB-CM (2012): 24.
134 EIB-CM (2012): 104–06.
135 EIB-CM (2012): 107.
136 EIB-CM (2012): 104.

the two healers together to finally settle their disputes failed again. Jaja Bujagali did not respond to the kingdom's invitation and refused to participate. Not only would the ritual be futile in his opinion, but he did not want to be treated as the equal of Nfuudu. On the contrary, Jaja Bujagali wanted to conduct his own ceremonies, which would involve very many spiritual healers from across Uganda at great cost.[137] As a consequence, in the absence of Jaja Bujagali, the ritual proceeded with Nfuudu. If the 2011 ritual was necessary to conduct because the 2007 ritual had been improper and not performed in an auspicious way, the same could be said of the latest ritual.

At the end of June 2011, Nfuudu again moved the Budhagaali spirit. The spiritual contestation between Jaja Bujagali and Nfuudu continued, and still does. In a newspaper article it was reported:

> The move, carried out last week, ended an impasse that had delayed the ritual for over three years … The conflict resulted in a stalemate until … Nfudu secured the blessings of the kingdom officials to conduct the event. The spirits were moved from the dam site to Namizi East village in Budondo sub-county in Jinja.[138]

Although Nfuudu claimed that the spirit resided in his compound, the ritual started by the river or the reservoir. As before, it was transported back to the new shrines in Namizi village, the place used in 2007 when the shrines were temporary. As the spirit was being moved for the third time, one must assume that it had been rather dissatisfied with the new shrines and at being moved around.

'We hereby certify that the construction of the shrines and associated features has now been completed to our satisfaction', states the Certificate of Completion of Namizi Shrines and Relocation of Budhagaali Spirits, signed by the Busoga kingdom and the government. According to Kawunhe Wakooli, acting *Kyabazinga* (king) of the Busoga kingdom:

> Today is an important day for Busoga and Uganda. Giving up our shrine [the waterfalls] was not easy – but for development's sake, we had to. The government should give our children jobs because the power project will benefit all of us. Busoga Kingdom should also get its fair share of the proceeds from the project.

Benedicto Nfuudu, the chief spirit medium, conducted the ritual. Standing in front of a smoking fire, he declared:

> Ever since the spirits were temporarily kept at my home after the ground breaking ceremony for the power dam, I have not had peace. They have been nagging me for another home … These new shrines are in honour of the Busoga. People will be coming here to worship the spirits of our dead who protect, direct and guide us. I pray and ask that the Busoga sacrifice a cow each year to appease the spirits.[139]

The contractor was also appeased.

---

137 EIB-CM (2012): 107.
138 Mugabi (2011).
139 Musinguzi (2011).

Where is the Budhagaali spirit?

The Budhagaali spirit has always remained in the river, or what is now the reservoir of the dam. All healers agree on this, apart from Nfuudu. Jaja Bujagali said that the river spirit was never moved in the 2007 ritual. All the spirits have been there all the time. Not only is the Budhagaali spirit still living in the waters, but so are innumerable other spirits and ancestors. As Jaja Bujagali pointed out, ordinary people are not supposed to direct and command the spirits; rather, the reverse is true. Consequently, the ritual initiated by the contractor and the government was improper. Similarly, when the medium is possessed, the spirit says what needs to be done and by whom – it is not for people to decide and say what the spirits should do.

Thus, throughout the whole process of construction, misconceptions about Busoga spirituality – and water spirits in particular – have led to many paradoxes, including the dam builder's attempts to remove the spirit, and activist claims that it would be destroyed. There is an inherent contradiction in the belief that a river god can be drowned by the construction of a dam. A river god can no more be destroyed than God or Jesus can be killed if a church is burnt down. Something as profane as a dam cannot destroy a god. In fact, it is impossible to drown a river spirit living in its own element. Moreover, residing in cascading waterfalls is a supreme manifestation of the powers of the spirit, but the waterfalls are *not* the spirit as such. Spirits are spirits and gods are gods, and their material embodiments and visualisations exist to allow humans to comprehend the divinities, but are not their essence. It is precisely because the Budhagaali spirit is a spirit that it is crucial for the whole of Busoga and not only for those living close to the river.

Religious aftermath and conclusion

Despite the fierce fighting among the healers and the kingdom's support for Nfuudu (which left Jaja Bujagali out in the cold), things have changed. The 2011 ritual was the last straw and changed the kingdom's attitude toward Nfuudu – simply because it was not a ritual. Afterwards he became persona non grata. Today, he is no longer the chief healer in the kingdom: a new healer has been appointed – one with no affiliation to the Bujagali Falls or the Budhagaali spirit. It is now generally acknowledged that the 2011 ritual was a staged, pretend ritual – a charade. Nfuudu was not possessed when the rite was performed, and the ritual did not convince participants. Consequently, Nfuudu was regarded as a charlatan and Jaja Bujagali was seen to have been right all along. The improper ritual performances convinced people that they had been deceived, and the kingdom realised it had been fooled by Nfuudu. It was impossible to transfer the spirit in the first place, and it was therefore impossible to transfer it either back or to the Namizi shrines.

Moreover, although it was claimed that Nfuudu moved the spirit in 2011, this claim was open to diverse interpretations. One is, of course, Nfuudu's version. Another

Figure 4.5. Jaja Bujagali in 2017, when he was 100 years old. Ten years after Nfuudu performed the ritual and five years after the dam was completed, the Budhagaali river spirit was still furious about the dam. Photo: Terje Oestigaard.

is that this is proof that if he relocated the spirit, it was not, by definition, in his possession – he was neither the owner of the spirit nor its incarnation. He could have been the custodian of the spirit for a short time, but he was not the proper Jaja Bujagali. Jaja Bujagali was the real and only medium of the Budhagaali spirit. Nfuudu was an imposter, and employing him as the healer for the rituals had had dire implications. The Budhagaali spirit was not pleased with what had happened. And when the kingdom realised that the 2011 ritual was a charade, the implication was that the rituals conducted in 2001 and 2007 had also been staged and were fake. Jaja Bujagali is the spirit's medium, and Nfuudu is a charlatan. Thus, the cosmological order has been restored – not to where it was before the dam project started (because so much water has 'flowed under the bridge', causing great upheavals) – but to the extent that Jaja Bujagali is the undisputed medium of the Budhagaali spirit. And that spirit is one of the most important in the Busoga cosmology.

Religion and indigenous culture have an important role to play in the World Bank's own guidelines, as the inspection panel recorded in 2008:

> The Panel notes that if the Busoga religion and cultural tradition had been … more fully understood and widely recognized …, the current site may not have been acceptable, or alternative sites would have been given … much stronger consideration.[140]

In other words, if the World Bank had properly understood the complicated processes at work at Bujagali Falls, it might have refused to support the dam, and the project might have been terminated once and for all – or at least until the Chinese entered the scene. Moreover, if there is one thing that the controversies surrounding the Bujagali Dam have shown, it is that religion and indigenous traditions are not something to be taken on lightly: for believers, it is a serious matter – not just a theatrical performance to please governments, sponsors or contractors; not just something that one needs to get through before proceeding with business as usual. However, there is another paradox with the Bujagali case. All three appeasement rituals were clearly invented traditions:[141] there never were such rituals in the past. As we have seen, it is questionable if they worked at all, or even functioned as part of the religious logic among the Busoga.

---

140 WB IP (2008): 174.
141 Hobsbawn and Ranger (1983), pp. 1-14.

References

Burnside (2006). *Bujagali Hydropower Project. Social and Environmental Assessment Report. Executive Summary*. R.J. Burnside International Limited, Canada, 2006.

Conca (2006). Conca, K. *Governing Water: Contentious transnational politics and global institution building*. MIT Press, Cambridge, Massachusetts, USA, 2006.

EIB-CM (2012). European Investment Bank Complaints Mechanism (EIB-CM). *Bujagali Hydroelectric Project, Jinja, Uganda. Complaint SG/E/2009/09. Conclusion Report*, 30 August 2012.

ERA (2012). *Electricity Regulatory Authority Newsletter, Issue 7*, December 2012.

Hobsbawn and Ranger (1983). Hobsbawn, E., and Ranger, T. (eds), *The Invention of Tradition*. Cambridge University Press, Cambridge, United Kingdom, 1983.

IAU (2010). Bujagali Hydropower Project (BHHP) *Witness NGO Annual Report 2010*. Inter Aid Uganda, Kampal, January-December 2010.

IDA (2008). *International Development Association, Report No. IDA/R2008-0296*. International Bank for Reconstruction and Development. International Development Association. Management Report and Recommendation in Response to the Inspection Panel Investigation Report, 2008.

Kitimbo (2007). Kitimbo, I. Uganda: Bujagali Spirits Relocated, *The Monitor*, 9 September 2007. http://allafrica.com/stories/200709100646.html (accessed 21 February 2014).

Lacey (2001). Lacey, M. Traditional Spirits Block a $500 Million Dam Plan in Uganda, *New York Times*, 13 September 2001. http://www.nytimes.com/2001/09/13/international/africa/13NILE.html (accessed 27 January 2014).

Mugabi (2011). Mugabi, F. Bujagali spirits moved to new place, *New Vision*, 6 July 2011, www.newvision.co.ug/new_vision/news/1008638/bujagali-spirits-moved (accessed 10 April 2014).

Musinguzi (2011). Musinguzi, B. 'Budhagali' water spirits find a new resting place, *The East African*, 24 July 2011. http://www.theeastafrican.co.ke/magazine/Budhagali+water+spirits+find+a+new+resting+place/-/434746/1206588/-/e6n3tvz/-/index.html (accessed 21 February 2014).

Oestigaard (2015). Oestigaard, Terje. *Dammed divinities: The water powers at Bujagali Falls, Uganda*, Current African Issues, No. 62. Nordic Africa Institute, Uppsala, Sweden, 2015.

Oweyegha-Afunaduula (2003). Oweyegha-Afunaduula, F.C. Huge dams as corporate crime and terrorism. *Nape Lobby*, 6th Edition, November 2003.

Oweyegha-Afunaduula and Isaac (2004). Oweyegha-Afunaduula, F.C., and Isaac, A. Environmental Hydropolitics of the Nile Basin's Bujagali Dam, Uganda: An Annotated Bibliography. Working to Protect River Nile, *Fighting for Justice Occasional Paper No. 7* NAPE/SBC-2004, 6 February 2004.

WB IP (2008). *World Bank Inspection Panel, Report No. 44977-UG*. The Inspection Panel. Investigation Report. Uganda: Private Power Generation (Bujagali) Project (Guarantee No. B0130-UG). August 29, 2008. World Bank, Washington, D.C., USA, 2008.

The private-sector approach would make firm power the most important outcome, and hence issues of agriculture, environ-ment and wildlife would be secondary.

/ Kjell Havnevik, p. 98

Tributary rivers Luwegu, Kilombero and Great Ruaha, winding through the Selous Game Reserve before they converge on the Stiegler's Gorge and flow onto the Lower Rufiji Flood Plain as Rufiji River. The artificial lake connected to the dam and hydropower project will be located inside the Game Reserve. Photo: BBM Explorer, Wikimedia.

Figure 5.1a. Location of the Rufiji River Basin in Tanzania. The Great Ruaha, the Kilombero and the Luwegu rivers bring water from four catchment areas. The rivers merge at Stiegler's Gorge into the major Rufiji River. Map illustration based on Shaghude 2016.

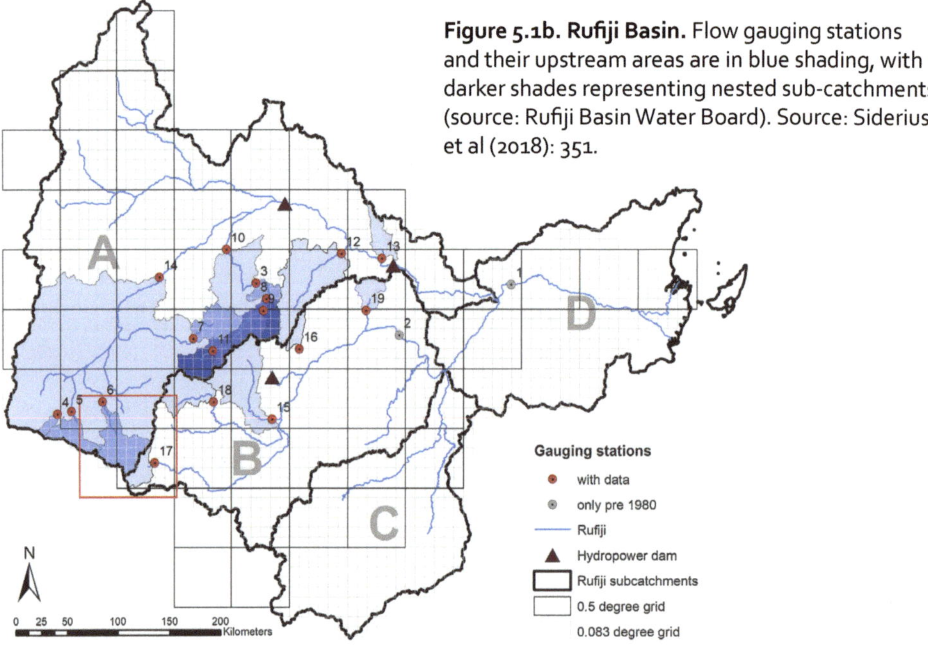

Figure 5.1b. Rufiji Basin. Flow gauging stations and their upstream areas are in blue shading, with darker shades representing nested sub-catchments (source: Rufiji Basin Water Board). Source: Siderius et al (2018): 351.

CHAPTER 5

The dam that was never built: The Stiegler's Gorge project in Tanzania

Kjell Havnevik

The Stiegler's Gorge project is the name given to a potential large dam and hydropower project located at Stiegler's Gorge in eastern Tanzania, on the edge of the Selous Game Reserve to the west and the Rufiji District to the east. Upstream from Stiegler's Gorge, three major rivers converge to form the Rufiji River, which – after passing through the gorge – flows into the Rufiji River valley and the cultivated Rufiji flood plain, before finally entering the Indian Ocean (having first bifurcated to create the Rufiji River delta). The implementation of the Stiegler's Gorge project will have major impacts both upstream (with the creation of a large lake as a resorvoir inside the Selous Game Reserve) and downstream – through a change in water flow in the Rufiji River over the year, which will affect agriculture in the Rufiji flood plain and the mangrove forests in the delta. Wildlife will be affected both in the Selous Game Reserve and parts of the upper river valley. Fishing activities will also be affected, both upstream and in the whole of the downstream area, including in adjacent waters of the Indian Ocean.

As long ago as 1904, Stiegler's Gorge was identified as the site for a major project by the German colonial state, which had taken control of the then Tanganyika around 1890. Since then, numerous studies have been carried out with the aim of developing the project, though its purpose has shifted over time.

Comprehensive studies and plans for initiating the project were drawn up in the early post-colonial decades of Tanzania. With the African crises of the early 1980s, the project was put on hold, and it was not until 2005 that new actors on the scene tried to mobilise to implement the project. However, to this day the Stiegler's Gorge project remains unfulfilled. Recently Tanzanian President Magufuli announced that the Stiegler's Gorge project will go ahead. But will he succeed? The Egyptian company Arab Contractors won the contract to build the Stiegler's Gorge Hydroelectric dam and project which will be carried out in partnership with Elsewedy Electric Company, also based in Egypt.[142]

---

142 Takouleu (2018).

This chapter will present the historical process involved in the planning of the Stiegler's Gorge project, in light of the changing domestic and international backdrop. The analysis will look into the orientation of the various planning initiatives and identify and analyse the causes and forces that have kept the project at the planning stage.

This chapter builds primarily on research conducted by the author into the project's planning process and its potential impact over time, with emphasis on the early phases of the project.[143] The later phase of the analysis, presented also in chapter 6, is mainly based on studies by other authors, including newspaper articles.[144]

Planning of Stiegler's Gorge during the colonial period

Way back in Tanganyika's colonial history, the Germans saw the potential for projects linked to Stiegler's Gorge. In 1904, 1907, 1909 and 1911, they undertook technical expeditions to the Rufiji Basin, in order to investigate the potential advantages of river navigation over rail transportation. A second objective was to examine the possibilities for irrigated agriculture and power production.[145] These investigations found rail transport to be more advantageous, since navigation was only possible on the lower reaches of the Rufiji River (and to a limited extent upstream, on the Kilombero River). However, no railway was built in the region by the Germans, and the dam and power station projects were also set aside. Germany lost its Tanganyika colony after its defeat in the First World War.

After the war, rule of Tanganyika was transferred to Great Britain, under the League of Nations mandate. It was the British who initiated the next major study of the Rufiji Basin – conducted in 1928/29 by Alexander Telford.[146] He took cross-sections of the river at various points; however, they were not related to sea level. He further put forward estimates for the potential agriculture without irrigation in the vicinity of the Kilombero and lower Rufiji rivers to be around 146,000 hectares, for the cultivation of rice, cotton and maize.

In 1940, a water consultant to the British Tanganyikan colonial government, Clement Gillman, stated that nothing was known about the flows of the main rivers, including the Rufiji. In spite of this, he advised the government that 'these rivers [do] not lend themselves to major schemes of irrigation or navigation which might justify the costs of gauging their flows'.[147] It seems evident that Gillman[148] consulted neither the important study by Marshland on agricultural cultivation in the lower Rufiji valley,[149]

---

143 Havnevik (1975); Havnevik (1978); Havnevik (1981); Havnevik (1982); Havnevik et al (1988) and Havnevik (1993).
144 Öhman, (2003); Hoag & Öhman (2008): 224-251 and Dye (2017).
145 Havnevik (1993): 263.
146 Telford (1929).
147 FAO (1961): 5.
148 Gillman (1945).
149 Marshland (1938): 55–59.

nor the Telford study of 1929. Gillman's advice had the effect of postponing systematic observation of river flows throughout Tanganyika.[150]

The next major study of the Rufiji Basin was initiated in the early 1950s by the then British governor of Tanganyika, who invited the United Nations Food and Agriculture Organization (FAO) to carry out a reconnaissance survey of the possibilities for development of the basin. The pilot study resulted in an interim report, published in 1954, which recommended that a major study should be undertaken, to include the investigation of soils, geology, topography and water control. This major study was published at the time of Tanganyika's independence, in 1961.[151]

The early German investigations and the subsequent studies of the Rufiji Basin (except Gillman's) recognised the multipurpose nature of a dam and power project at Stiegler's Gorge. Such a project would have an impact on wildlife, power production, agriculture, fishing and forestry alike, including on the fragile ecological system of the Rufiji delta.[152]

In addition to the local impacts, the Stiegler's Gorge project was bound to loom large in the national economy. This was partly related to the potential for electric power and agricultural production; but it also had to do with the fact that funding for such a major project would imply limitations on support for other development projects in the country.

The early phases of post-independence planning

The major preoccupation of the government of post-independence Tanganyika (which merged with Zanzibar in 1964 to become Tanzania) was modernisation of the economy and consolidation of the state. However, at the time of independence, no social group or class was strong enough to impose its interests on the state formation. This provided a basic underpinning of the nationalist ideology that the state was a state for all. The state assumed the role of lead actor and agent of the modernisation process, which aimed at economic growth and increased fulfilment of everybody's basic needs.

At independence, a fundamental issue was the modernisation of agricultural development through irrigation schemes – clearly stated in the Tanzanian First Three Year Plan 1961-1964.[153] This idea had also been promoted by the British colonial government, which outlined the terms of reference of the FAO study into the Rufiji Basin that was initiated in the mid-1950s and published in 1961.[154] This study was to focus on the control of water to improve land utilisation; the question of hydropower was not raised. Nevertheless, the study stated that power production would be technically feasible, and hydroelectric power could be generated on a considerable scale through the construction

---

150 FAO (1961).
151 FAO (1961).
152 See Havnevik (1993): 264-265 and chapters 4 and 5.
153 Öhman (2003): 12.
154 FAO (1961).

of dams at Stiegler's Gorge (150-400 MW) and at Mtera (21 MW) on the Great Ruaha River. However, the study emphasised that only by considering the future power requirements of Tanganyika as a whole could it be determined whether such developments were likely to be justifiable. In addition, the study mentioned that minor and varying amounts of power could be generated at a number of dams proposed primarily for the control of rivers. The study stated that there was a clear trade-off between agricultural and power production. The cost of irrigation (£50 per acre for the potentially irrigated area) was considered high. If the full cost of a dam had to be charged to agriculture, the project appeared uneconomic. But if the reservoir created could also cater for reliable hydropower production, perhaps half (or even less) of the cost could be charged to flood control and irrigation, which would make the project viable.[155]

The subsequent study on the Rufiji Basin initiated by the post-colonial Tanzanian government was conducted by the US Department of the Interior's Bureau of Reclamation. It was prepared for USAID and was presented to the Tanzanian government in 1967.[156] Its terms of reference were to undertake a review of the existing data and studies on the Rufiji Basin and to suggest guidelines for the possible formation of a Rufiji Basin Development Authority – RUBADA (eventually established by an act of parliament in 1975). The study, however, also shifted the focus of subsequent studies in the direction of hydropower, by stating that:

> Before proceeding on a large-scale development of hydro-electric energy, Stiegler's Gorge should be fully evaluated. This evaluation should include determination of the optimum amount of storage at the site and upstream storage which would provide regulation. Location and arrangements of generating plants to develop the maximum available head at Stiegler's Gorge should be studied.[157]

Simultaneously, the Overseas Technical Cooperation Agency of the Japanese Government (JETRO), carried out a pre-feasibility study of the Stiegler's Gorge hydroelectric project, with the primary objective of developing hydropower for industrial expansion. It concluded that the Stiegler's Gorge hydropower project was viable; that it should include transmission lines at an estimated cost of USD 121 million (1968); and that 600 MW could be installed in the project. But the generation of such large amounts of hydropower would necessitate a programme of industrialisation in Tanzania, including an aluminium smelting works.

No formal documents exist to indicate that the Tanzanian government accepted JETRO's recommendation on the Stiegler's Gorge project.[158] However, soon after the finalisation of the JETRO study, the Tanzanian government did ask the United Nations Development Programme (UNDP) for assistance in undertaking a feasibility study of the Stiegler's Gorge hydropower project. Nothing materialised from this request, but a few

---

155 FAO (1961): 41 and Havnevik (1993): 266–67.
156 USAID (1967).
157 USAID (1967): 160.
158 Nkonoki (1983).

years later the Norwegian Agency for Development Cooperation (NORAD) was asked to assist in the planning of the Stiegler's Gorge project. NORAD came to be engaged in the planning of Stiegler's Gorge project from 1970 until the mid-1980s – nearly 15 years.

NORAD contracted Norconsult to conduct a study of the Stiegler's Gorge project, and a preliminary report was published in 1972. Norconsult acknowledged the multipurpose character of the Lower Rufiji Basin Development and the Stiegler's Gorge project. But in spite of that, the report stated that it would deal primarily with the hydropower aspect of the project: the other aspects would be regarded as secondary. This approach corresponded well, however, to the terms of reference of the study, which simply asked Norconsult to prepare a preliminary project for a dam and a power station, and to come up with realistic costs for the electric energy produced.[159]

Norconsult's study rested on the assumption that flood control and irrigation would not lead to a net income for the project in the near future. Therefore, the sale of energy to power-consuming industries constituted its financial base.[160] Following this, Norconsult concluded that the optimal size of the dam and its highest regulated water level – elements that are closely related to the multipurpose character of the project – were chosen with the aim of optimising one single purpose: power production. The highest regulated water level was thus set at a level that gave the lowest variable unit cost for the electricity provided by the project – 178 metres above sea level.[161]

Norconsult concluded that the hydropower project could be developed with a power unit cost that was economic for power-consuming industries. Since no local market existed for full consumption of the power generated by the project at the time or in the near future, Norconsult strongly recommended establishing power-consuming industries, in order to create demand for the electricity produced by the project. The consultants calculated the firm power production capacity of the project at 620 MW, and only firm power would be of value to power-consuming industries.

The preliminary study by Norconsult was followed by a study by another Norwegian company – Hafslund A/S (and also funded by NORAD). The terms of reference of this study indicated that the planning perspective continued to be limited, although some consideration was given to the project's multipurpose nature. The major items in the study's terms of reference included: (i) supply of electrical energy at competitive prices for bulk delivery to the Tanzanian electric supply company TANESCO, for delivery to power-consuming industries and for other purposes; (ii) the establishment of effective flood control, in order to improve conditions for agriculture in the Lower Rufiji Basin, including infrastructure in the area; (iii) a further improvement in agriculture downstream, through irrigation schemes; and (iv) improvement in fishing in the artificial lake created by the water reservoir, as well as fisheries in the river.[162]

Despite the fact that the terms of reference emphasised the multipurpose nature of the project, the instructions for the study's planning of hydropower production

159 Norconsult (1972).
160 Norconsult (1972): 63.
161 Norconsult (1972).
162 ToR (1976), para 1.4.

Figure 5.2. Workers at Stiegler's Gorge, September 1978. Photo: Kjell Havnevik.

were formulated thus: 'The project shall be planned with the main object of maximum power production. Consideration shall however also be paid to the demand for flood control and irrigation in the Lower Rufiji Basin.' This was clearly contradictory: concern for the demand for flood control to enhance irrigated agriculture would not allow maximum power production, based on the highest possible water level in the reservoir. And in addition, the terms of reference stated that the Tanzanian government would prepare a general programme for the agricultural development of the lower Rufiji flood plain through flood control and irrigation.[163]

However, RUBADA never provided such a programme, and so the water requirement for agriculture could not be ascertained. Hafslund therefore hired its own consultants to address the downstream issues, in order to verify the preliminary design criteria of the dam. A crucial parameter in the design of the dam was the capacity of its lower-level outlets. Since the transformation from a flood-adapted to an artificially irrigated agricultural system would require time, these outlets had to be designed to release adequate water to create floods downstream. Hafslund's preliminary design for a minimum capacity of 2,500 cubic metres per second for the low-level outlets was deemed satisfactory by the consultants, who stated that this volume of water discharge would create extensive flooding on the downstream river plain.

When Hafslund presented its preliminary project in Dar es Salaam in January 1979, it claimed that the Stiegler's Gorge could not withstand the release of more than

---

163 ToR (1976), para 5.

2,500 cubic metres per second, due to problems of erosion in the gorge. Consequently, if more water were needed for flooding downstream, it would have to be taken from the spillways of the saddle dams. Given these conditions, the release of 2,500 cubic metres per second from the low-level spillways of the main dam must be seen as a maximum, rather than a minimum.

However, when Hafslund conducted its study (mainly during 1978 and 1979), no adequate studies had been made of the agricultural potential of the downstream area, of flood control benefits, and of alternative ways of obtaining flood control. Hafslund could therefore not properly reflect the multipurpose nature of the project in its planning, as the necessary data were simply not available.

Uneven development of major areas of the project

Already in 1977, a growing anxiety had developed among concerned parties about the uneven development of major areas of the planning of the project. It was realised that the technical design of the project would be finalised before adequate studies had been conducted on critical issues of the use of hydropower and the downstream effects in Rufiji District and the adjacent Indian Ocean. This led to a frenetic process of initiating additional analyses of the demand for electricity, in order to make the project appear bankable and to make the aspects of downstream planning better match the project's multipurpose nature.

Figure 5.3. Stiegler's Gorge, September 1978. Tanzanian workers and Norwegian engineers at the head of a tunnel – investigating the geological formation at the site of the dam. Photo: Kjell Havnevik.

Before 1979, the discussions between NORAD and the Tanzanian government had not focused on the financing aspects of the project's implementation. NORADs project coordinator in 1972 Bjørn Lunøe had tried to stop the project design development at a stage when it would be possible to provide a reliable cost estimate, to be used to initiate the process of project funding (personal communication in 1992). However, the Tanzanian minister responsible deferred to strong political pressure from the government, and argued that there would be no problem with financing the project. He urged NORAD to go ahead and finalise the project design; and NORAD agreed to do so.

The demand for electricity

Uncertainty about the demand for electricity had all along plagued the development of the Stiegler's Gorge project. The fear was that – even from a narrow hydropower perspective – the project would not appear feasible. TANESCO thus gave the Canadian firm Acres International Ltd the task of preparing a power generation development master plan up to the year 1995, which was to be used as the basis for the planning of the Stiegler's Gorge project. The preliminary Acres report estimated that by 1995, only 225 MW additional capacity would be required in Tanzania. Since it was envisaged that the Stiegler's Gorge project would provide between 600 and 1,000 MW to come on stream toward the end of the 1980s, Acres concluded that alternative options to provide power should be investigated, and that the Stiegler's Gorge project should be given very low priority. Commissioning of the Stiegler's Gorge project would only be feasible if major non-power benefits were linked to the project.

The Tanzanian government rejected these recommendations and sought advice from other sources. In 1978, two other studies forecasting electricity demand in Tanzania had been initiated: one by RUBADA, conducted by George Joseph of the University of Dar es Salaam's Department of Statistics, and one jointly by the Ministry of Industries and the Ministry of Water, Energy and Minerals. The latter forecast analysis was executed by M.D. Segal, an advisor to the Ministry of Industries, and S.L. Mosha of TANESCO.

In his report, Joseph strongly criticised the approach of the Acres (1978) study, claiming among other things that its point predictions, based on a single future growth rate of GDP were unsatisfactory. Interval predictions based on assumptions of low-, medium- and high-growth scenarios would be more realistic.[164] He further claimed that Acres had not taken account of the fact that different types of industries would have different requirements for electrical energy. Joseph expected a dramatic increase in demand for electricity in Tanzania, based on the National Development Corporation's (NDC) estimate that in ten years the iron/steel complex would require 75 MW, the paper and pulp complex another 21 MW (which would triple over time) and furthermore, sugar projects, textiles, ginneries, foundries and machinery, etc. would take up

---

164 Joseph (1979): 14.

another 60–75 MW. In ten years, industries along the TAZARA railway (linking the port of Dar es Salaam with the town of Kapiri Mposhi in Zambia's Central Province) would require 200 MW.[165] His overall conclusion was that by the year 2000, Tanzania would require an additional 670 MW, in addition to what was installed by TANES-CO in 1979. Hence the increased electricity produced by the Stiegler's Gorge project would be utilised in the longer term.[166] These findings thus played well into the hands of the promoters of the Stiegler's Gorge project.

The downstream multipurpose issues

The nature of Stiegler's Gorge also required flood control and irrigation to be integrated into the planning of the project. In addition, the overall impact on fisheries, forestry (primarily mangroves in the Rufiji delta), transport, health and ecology came to be included in the downstream issues. Upstream from the dam, issues were raised and discussed – for instance, regarding the need to rescue animals from the reservoir to be created; the impact of a construction camp with some 25,000 persons; and a possible permanent settlement in the Selous Game Reserve.

RUBADA – which was to be responsible for providing most of the studies – had only been created in 1975. The institution was still weak in terms of manpower and competence when the terms of reference of the Hafslund study of the Stiegler's Gorge project were drawn up, in 1976. In outlining the body's functioning, the 1975 RUBA-DA Act covers all the multipurpose aspects related to the planning and implementation of the Stiegler's Gorge project.

For its part, the University of Dar es Salaam (UDSM) – and in particular its Bureau of Resource Assessment and Land Use Planning (BRALUP) (now the Institute of Resource Assessment) – had over time conducted a number of studies related to the downstream issues of relevance to the Stiegler's Gorge project. These included a study on soils[167] and on the socio-economic system of the inner delta areas.[168] In addition, the Ministry of Water Development and Power had commissioned a study of the productive system of the Rufiji Valley, conducted in the 1970/71 agricultural season.[169]

Using data he had collected through extensive field studies in the lower delta,[170] the anthropologist Audun Sandberg, based at BRALUP/IRA, criticised Norconsult's approach in its pre-feasibility study.[171] Other studies pointed to weaknesses in the Norconsult study and to the need for adjustments to it, so that planning could be carried forward in a multipurpose context.[172]

---

165 Joseph (1979): 16.
166 Joseph (1979): 41-42.
167 Cook (1974).
168 Sandberg (1973); Angwazi and Ndulu (1973).
169 Yoshida (1974).
170 Sandberg (1974a) and Sandberg (1974b).
171 Norconsult (1972).
172 Havnevik (1975) and Havnevik (1978).

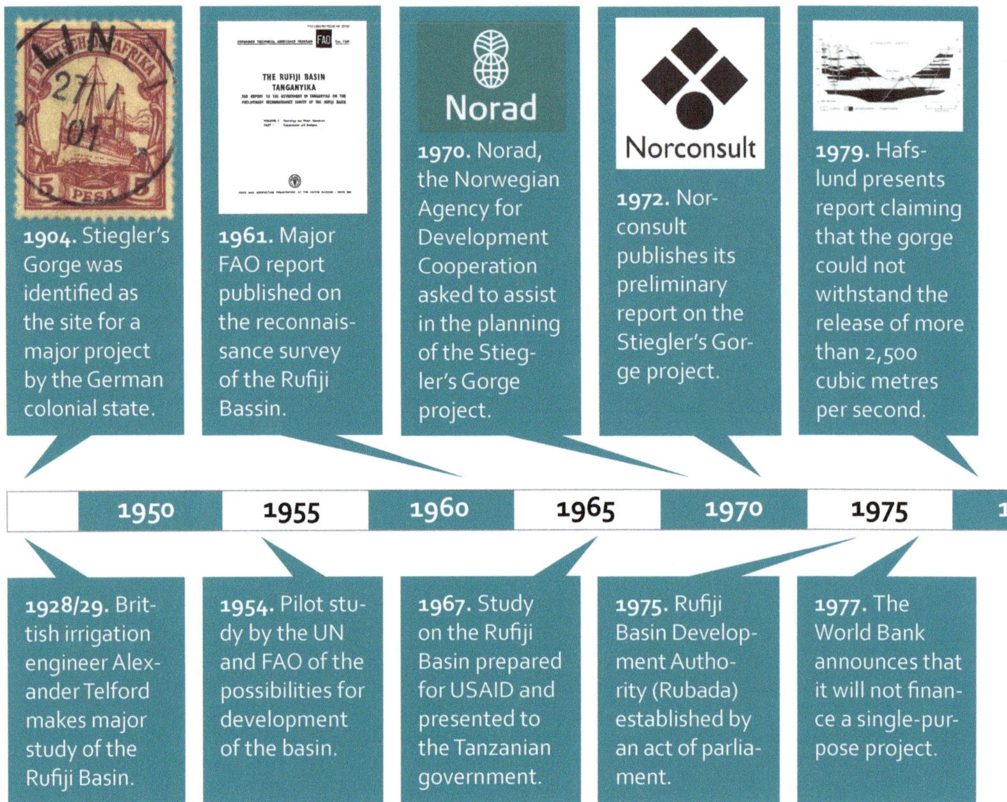

These criticisms of the Stiegler's Gorge planning process had been communicated to NORAD prior to the preparation of the terms of reference for the Hafslund study, in 1976. Criticism of the planning process had also developed inside NORAD. The impact of this criticism on the direction of planning was, however, marginal. Further criticism of the planning process emerged during 1977 and 1978. However, NORAD's attitude did not change much until the World Bank let it be known that a single-purpose project would not be financed by the institution. All of a sudden, it dawned on the stakeholders of the project that a multipurpose approach to the planning of the project was essential for its successful funding and implementation.

Attempts to rectify the project planning process

When the World Bank dropped its bombshell, NORAD acted. Toward the end of 1977, a high-level delegation from the Norwegian Ministry of Foreign Affairs and NORAD visited Tanzania (and met President Julius Nyerere) to persuade the Tanzanian authorities to take seriously the need for a broader multipurpose approach to the planning of the Stiegler's Gorge project. This would also require much a higher priority for RUBADA,

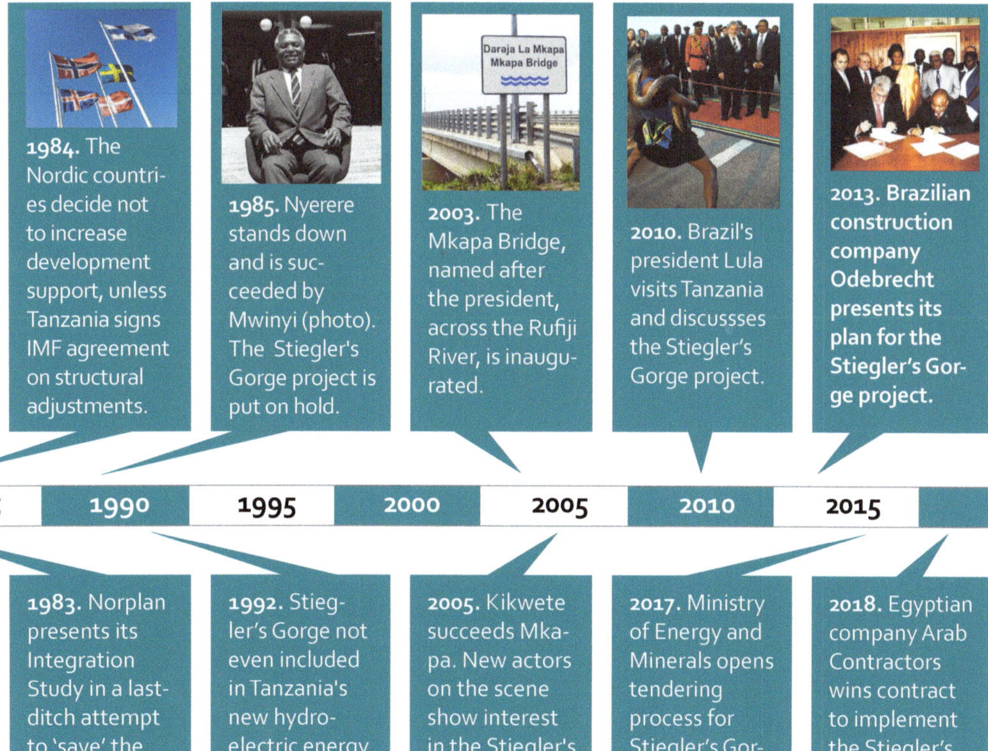

1984. The Nordic countries decide not to increase development support, unless Tanzania signs IMF agreement on structural adjustments.

1985. Nyerere stands down and is succeeded by Mwinyi (photo). The Stiegler's Gorge project is put on hold.

2003. The Mkapa Bridge, named after the president, across the Rufiji River, is inaugurated.

2010. Brazil's president Lula visits Tanzania and discussses the Stiegler's Gorge project.

2013. Brazilian construction company Odebrecht presents its plan for the Stiegler's Gorge project.

85 | 1990 | 1995 | 2000 | 2005 | 2010 | 2015

1983. Norplan presents its Integration Study in a last-ditch attempt to 'save' the project.

1992. Stiegler's Gorge not even included in Tanzania's new hydro-electric energy policy.

2005. Kikwete succeeds Mkapa. New actors on the scene show interest in the Stiegler's Gorge project.

2017. Ministry of Energy and Minerals opens tendering process for Stiegler's Gorge project.

2018. Egyptian company Arab Contractors wins contract to implement the Stiegler's Gorge project.

as the major coordinating agency for the impact studies. However, NORAD was also careful to stress that its commitment to the project was only to the planning phase, and there was no assurance of support for funding of the project. The actions of NORAD, however, also indicated its interest in the project's implementation, for which Norwegian companies (which by that time had nearly completed the construction of all potential dams and hydropower projects in Norway) would be available.

The most critical aspect of restoring the multipurpose nature of the project planning was the series of impact studies in the downstream areas of Stiegler's Gorge. In January 1978, a new NORAD delegation visited Tanzania. This time, the aim was to promote an environmental impact assessment (EIA) of the Stiegler's Gorge project, in conjunction with RUBADA and the University of Dar es Salaam. Some progress was made, and RUBADA and the university were able to formulate large sections of an EIA document; however, organisational issues were left for a later stage. NORAD took on a role as mediator between the Tanzanian institutions, and guaranteed the funding of the EIA programme. However, problems arose when more concrete formulations of the EIA were required, including priorities and organisational issues. Those participants in the process from the UDSM (including myself, under contract to BRALUP from 1978 to 1980 and funded by NORAD) became aware that there was a conflict about the focus of the impact studies and whose interests they should serve.

The bureaucratic promoters of the project in Tanzania – RUBADA and a group of officials within NORAD – became irritated by the position and arguments of the UDSM researchers. They also blamed the university for not having a unified leadership that could build momentum and see the impact studies carried out. In this they were partly correct – relations between key personnel within the university could hardly have been termed cordial, and the same was true of relations between various Tanzanian institutions that were involved. But real disagreement as to the choice of perspectives for the EIA also played an important part in the breakdown of cooperation between RUBADA and the UDSM. A strong faction within NORAD also started to argue, alongside RUBADA, that the university was unable to deliver the impact studies on time. Hence, it would be necessary to involve and contract international consultants to get the EIA studies completed. NORAD personnel and Tanzanians who opted for a more local approach to conducting the studies that would also enhance the long-term competence of Tanzanian personnel and researchers became frustrated and withdrew from the discussions.

Three different sets of impact studies subsequently appeared. The major part of the NORAD funding was channelled to international consultants. In a second strand of studies, RUBADA to a limited extent contracted Tanzanian (including university) personnel to conduct impact studies. A third strand was represented by the continuation of the UDSM studies that had been undertaken primarily by BRALUP since the early 1970s. Although the perspectives of the latter studies were often wider than the potential impact of the Stiegler's Gorge project, they were still relevant for generating knowledge regarding the impact of the project in one way or another.

In sum, what was intended as a major programme of environmental impact assessment that would enhance the long-term capacity and competence of Tanzanian institutions and personnel, ended up as a more or less closed circuit, comprising external consultants (who conducted the impact studies), RUBADA (the agency for project implementation) and NORAD. Relevant university input on Rufiji was marginalised.

When Hafslund presented its draft report on the Stiegler's Gorge project in November 1979, concerned representatives from some UDSM departments requested and were allowed to participate in the discussions. However, when more sensitive issues of the Stiegler's Gorge project were to be dealt with, the university representatives were asked to leave. It became clear, however, that the assistant to the director-general of RUBADA, Jac Smit, an expatriate US national who was funded by NORAD, had also developed a negative attitude to the planning of the project. This could be observed during the open session, when the director-general of RUBADA tried to keep his involvement to a minimum. Instead, the director-general relied on another expatriate expert working on contract in the Ministry of Industries and co-author of one of the electricity demand forecasts mentioned earlier, Mr M.D. Segal.

After some adjustments and updating, in July 1980 Hafslund, in cooperation with Norplan (another Norwegian company contracted for support), presented the final

Stiegler's Gorge Power and Flood Control Development, Project Planning Report. In Havnevik (1993, appendix 3: 337-338) an overview of the 27 impact related studies is given. Of these, 18 of the most strategic and resource demanding had been conducted by international consultants. Of the nine reports from Tanzanian institutions, two were produced by RUBADA, three by UDSM staff and four by the staff of other Tanzanian institutions. Only a few of the external study authors (for example, the Norwegian River and Harbour Laboratories) had an effective working relationship with their Tanzanian counterparts during the process. Rather than conducting field studies, it was more common for many of the external consultants to appropriate the research material produced by the relevant Tanzanian institutions and just reproduce it, often without any proper credits.

However, what turned out to be extremely damaging for the evaluation of the Hafslund Final Project Planning Report was that more than half, including the most important ones, of the impact related studies were not finalized at the time of presentation of the Hafslund Final Planning Report in 1980.[173] Hence their analyses and findings could only have limited or no influence on the technical and economic aspects of the final project design of the dam.

Major potential funders of the Stiegler's Gorge project did not find the planning process satisfactory from a multipurpose planning perspective. Hence, funding for the project was not forthcoming. Another factor that influenced funding was the deepening economic and social crisis that had emerged in Tanzania and Africa toward the end of the 1970s, in parallel with the stagnation of the global economy. In 1979, Tanzania also ran into serious disagreements with the International Monetary Fund (IMF) as to the path forward in economic reforms.[174] In fact, the head of the IMF mission to Tanzania was expelled from the country by the president of Tanzania during the mission's visit to Tanzania in 1979. Tanzania instead tried to move forward with the World Bank and likeminded countries, including Norway, the other Nordic countries and the Netherlands. However, in 1984, the Nordic countries informed Tanzania that there would be no option for increased development assistance support, unless the country signed an agreement about structural adjustment with the IMF.[175] Evidently, the conditions for the funding of a large-scale project such as Stiegler's Gorge had already deteriorated drastically when Hafslund/Norplan presented its final report, in July 1980.

In spite of these developments, a last-ditch attempt was made to 'save' the Stiegler's Gorge project by its promoters. This initiative was also funded by NORAD and executed by the Norwegian company Norplan, in association with Mr M.D. Segal. The final report, presented in August 1983, bore the title *The Lower Rufiji Valley Integration Study* (henceforth the Integration Study). The two main objectives of the study were: (i) to outline a final overall assessment of the Stiegler's Gorge Power and Flood Control Development, with a view to determining whether or not it was worth constructing

---

173 See Havnevik (1993), Appendix 3. This overview is based on NORPLAN 1983, Vol I, Appendix E, the so-called Integration Study.

174 Wangwe (1987).

175 Gibbon, Havnevik and Hermele (1993).

the dam and associated works; and (ii) to draw up a long-term integrated plan for the optimal development of the resources of the lower Rufiji Basin. This plan was expected to focus on the integrated development of the area, with an assumption that the hydropower project would eventually be realised. Given the long lead time of an undertaking as large as the Stiegler's Gorge power project, the plan was also to identify viable projects suitable for capital financing within the next five years, regardless of the dam project (Volume 1). The objective of the Integration Study was to review and pull together the findings and recommendations of the various studies already conducted into one single, integrated analysis.

By agreement with RUBADA, Norplan contracted responsibility for Part I – 'The Overall Assessment' – to Mr M.D. Segal, while the part dealing with development programmes and physical impacts was contracted to an Irish consultancy. Nearly all the major actors in the Integration Study had earlier been part of the planning of the project connected to the Hafslund study.[176] If the objective (to me a reasonable one) had been to improve the project planning through the sound integration of sub-studies and a critical analysis of the work already done, a different approach would have been required: an independent group of experts should have taken a fresh look at past project planning, including the potential for the integration of various parts or aspects, with a view to identifying potential macro-economic obstacles created by recent developments, both domestic and international. Instead, NORAD decided in 1982 to contract Norplan and to accept the participation of Mr. M.D. Segal in a major part of the study. This implied that 'vested interests' of the past planning process were once more called upon to 'save' the Stiegler's Gorge project.

Some of the technical reasons why this approach did not succeed were related to the treatment of the flood control and low-level outlets of the dam. A study by Agrar and Hydrotechnik (1982) stated that fully irrigated development downstream should be designed with a 1:100 year assurance against uncontrolled flooding. When this condition was built into the flood frequency simulations, it emerged that a controlled flood of 4,000 cubic metres per second would be optimal. Compared to the Hafslund finding (1980), this implied a 60 per cent increase of the release capacity of the low-level outlets at Stiegler's Gorge. The Integration Study was, however, of the opinion that expanding the capacity of the low-level outlets to 3,000 cubic metres per second would be sufficient to address the 1:100 year flood security. The additional 1,000 cubic metres per second were expected to come from the discharge of the turbines and, after phase III of the project, additional controlled release facilities through the gated spillway, when reservoir levels were above 174 metres.[177]

There are two major problems that could undermine the above calculations. First, the simulations on the power production and flood control programme – TANZA – were based on run-off data for only the 22 years from 1956 to 1978.[178] It is understandable that the Hafslund/Norplan report from 1980 did not utilise flood data beyond

---

176 Havnevik (1993): 280.
177 Agrar and Hydrotechnik (1982), vol. 1: 11-12.
178 Norplan (1983): Vol. 1, Appendix A: A6.

1978. The Integration Study did, however, have ample opportunity to do so, since it was published in August 1983. In that case, the 1979 flood – probably the largest of the twentieth century – would have been included: that flood exceeded 11,000 cubic metres per second at Stiegler's Gorge.[179] Taking this flood into account would probably have cast doubt on the conclusion that a capacity of 4,000 cubic metres per second at low-level outlets was sufficient to ensure 1:100 year security against uncontrolled flooding. Thus, the Integration Study overlooked available data which could have strengthened the reliability of the TANZA simulations. Poor flood control simulations would clearly lead to a higher probability of the destruction of investments in irrigation agriculture in the lower Rufiji River flood plain (and in other investments that had been undertaken due to the sense of increased security from downstream floods that emerged after construction of the dam).

Secondly, no historical analysis of the land use of the catchment area was linked to the development of the floods. This would have been required for an understanding of the impact of non-physical factors on flood profiles over time.[180] Hence, the TANZA simulations did not use available data and did not analyse flood data in a relevant manner: a 1:100 year security against uncontrolled flooding is likely to require in excess of even the projected 4,000 cubic metres per second capacity at the low-level outlets.

The capacity of the low-level outlets and the way it relates to erosion of the gorge is another major problem in the approach of the Integration Study. It was pointed out by Hafslund that 2,500 cubic metres per second were regarded as the maximum low-level release, due to erosion problems in the gorge. The Integration Study, however, stated that the technical review panel (no. 5) supported an increase in the capacity of the low-level outlets, because it would decrease the frequency with which the spillway structure needed to be operated and would add flexibility to the operation of the reservoir. But what about the panel's judgement on the impact of erosion in the wake of the increased capacity of the low-level dam outlets? Was the panel ignorant of Hafslund's warning? It seems that the increase in capacity of the low-level outlets recommended by the Integration Study is not advisable.

As for the estimate of electricity demand, the Integration Study emphasised that this was of fundamental importance to an evaluation of the cost-effectiveness of supply alternatives.[181] The Integration Study, which was carried out in 1982/83, adopted the July 1981 TANESCO forecast for electricity demand. However, during the work on the Integration Study, Tanzania was suffering a severe economic crisis. This drastically affected industrial production and the industrial load, which, according to the Integration Study, accounted 'for about two-thirds of electric consumption in Tanzania, hence a major emphasis of the forecast is on the expected evolution of the industrial load'.[182] By early 1983, all the major stakeholders with responsibility for undertaking the Integration Study knew that industrial production in the country had declined

179 Havnevik (1993): 281.
180 See Havnevik (1993): chapter 4.
181 Norplan (1983): Vol. 1: 14.
182 Norplan (1983): Vol. 1: 15.

dramatically in 1981 and 1982, and that the decline was expected to continue during 1983 and beyond. Why did the Integration Study team not attempt to adjust TANES-CO's July 1981 forecast (which they utilised in the study) to a more realistic level? One reason, given by the Integration Study itself, is that a large amount of work would have been required to construct well-grounded short-term forecast alternatives.[183] The development of reliable forecasts for electricity demand is, however, of critical importance for the Stiegler's Gorge project, whose economic and social viability was strongly connected to the future demand for electricity. On this account, in my view the approach of the Integration Study is irresponsible.

The Integration Study's treatment of flood control and security and of electricity demand thus casts serious doubts on its credibility. The whole exercise of the Integration Study seemed futile even from the very beginning, due to the major economic crisis in the Tanzanian economy, and given the poor state of the African and international economies. The attempt by the Integration Study to 'save' the Stiegler's Gorge project by presenting what was thought to be a sound and modified project thus failed.

From the early 1970s until well into the 1980s, NORAD was a staunch supporter of the project and invested around NOK 150 million in its planning.[184] Because of this investment, only very limited Tanzanian capacity and competence were developed: the main beneficiaries were international consultancies, primarily based in Norway. Of course, Norwegian companies were also interested in the future potential contracts that could emerge from implementation of the project. Pressure on NORAD from the Norwegian hydropower lobby would seem to be the only sensible explanation for why the agency pursued the planning process in such an awkward way. But there was one other reason. At the time of the high-level Norwegian delegation's visit to Tanzania in 1977, connected to the potential problems of funding of the Stiegler's Gorge project, Tanzanian President Julius Nyerere informed the Norwegian delegation that he wished all Norwegian development assistance to be channelled toward implementation of the Stiegler's Gorge project. Hence, NORAD could argue that in fact it had consulted the top political echelons of Tanzania, including the president, about the recipient country's wishes as regards implementation of the Stiegler's Gorge project.

A subsequent survey from 1985 of suitable hydropower projects to be developed in Tanzania showed, not unexpectedly, that Stiegler's Gorge was low on the priority list.[185] The energy policy of Tanzania published in 1992 did not even include the Stiegler's Gorge project among the six new hydroelectric projects to be developed in the next project generation.[186]

---

183 Norplan (1983): Vol. 1: 14.
184 Havnevik et al (1988).
185 Havnevik et al (1988): 265.
186 URT (1992).

Recent phases in the post-independence planning

After a long dormant period, interest in the planning and implementation of the Stiegler's Gorge project was reactivated by President Jakaya Kikwete, who was elected president after Benjamin Mkapa in 2005. President Mkapa had left his imprint on Rufiji District, due to his successive efforts to get the government to construct the Rufiji River bridge, which was inaugurated in 2003. This bridge provides better access to the southern part of Rufiji District, which could earlier only be reached by ferry via the river. It also improved road travel and transport from Dar es Salaam to the southern regions of the country, where Mkapa himself hailed from. On the other hand, it also made easier the exploitation of forest to the south of the river and beyond, due to better access to the major Dar es Salaam market.

The upturn in the Tanzanian economy in the new millennium was reflected in the Kikwete administration's optimism, and a major priority that emerged in this connection was the rehabilitation and expansion of projects for the provision of power. Furthermore, after a drought-induced power crisis that affected the country between 2004 and 2006, a number of longstanding projects that had never materialised reappeared on the government agenda, including Stiegler's Gorge. In order to move the Stiegler's Gorge project forward, the government strengthened RUBADA in terms of both manpower and funding, thus allowing it to take a more proactive stance. The efforts to identify and secure an international partner for the project were also shared by the wider government circles.[187]

Several international companies also took an interest in the Stiegler's Gorge project, but it was not until 2009/10 that plans became more concrete. The actor that somewhat unexpectedly entered the stage was the Brazilian construction company Odebrecht. This was connected to the Brazilian government's desire to make the country's presence felt more keenly both economically and internationally. Brazil had by then had nearly a decade of economic upturn. Brazilian companies, including Odebrecht, were not new to Africa, but they had primarily been operating in Angola and other former Portuguese colonies.

In 2009, Brazil appointed an ambassador to Tanzania, and President Luiz Inácio Lula da Silva (or simply Lula) visited the country the following year. The Stiegler's Gorge project was then discussed at a high level by Tanzanian ministries, Brazilian government representatives and senior Odebrecht executives. Odebrecht had long experience of large-scale construction of buildings, roads, dams and various other projects, and had built up a strong reputation beyond Brazil and Latin America. The Brazilian-Tanzanian relationship was further bolstered by a number of visits to Brazil by Tanzanian ministers and the president between 2010 and 2013. A Memorandum of Understanding (MoU) was signed by the parties in July 2012. Odebrecht acted quickly, and as early as in 2013 the company presented its plan for implementation of the Stiegler's Gorge project.[188]

---

187 Dye (2017): 1.
188 Odebrecht (2013).

Odebrecht proposed to construct a project with the capacity to generate 2,096 MW, providing 6,000 gigawatt hours (GWh) of firm energy per year. Figures from the 2015 Tanzanian National Energy Policy state that the country had installed generation capacity of 1,483 MW, but additional installations were likely to have pushed the capacity to 1,750 MW. Annual electricity consumption in 2014 was around 4,200 GWh. According to Odebrecht's plan, the Stiegler's Gorge project would more than double the country's total power generation capacity, and would supply 50 per cent more energy than the country was consuming in 2014.

As in the 1970s, the government presented estimates that would make a reasonable case for the project being implemented. The Power Systems Master Plan of 2009 estimated that in 2033 the peak demand would be 35,000 GWh and generation capacity 6,100 MW. In this longer-term context, there would be no problem in utilising the additional capacity installed at Stiegler's Gorge. Also, the argument went, Stiegler's Gorge power would represent the lowest-cost option for Tanzania (investment per kilowatt hour), and the power would be firm and based on known – and renewable – technologies.

The cost of the project was estimated by Odebrecht at USD 3.6 billion – far beyond Tanzania's own financial capability (total government expenditure in 2015/16 was USD 12 billion). Hence, Odebrecht proposed that funding for the project should come from a consortium that invested in the construction of the project; it would recover its investment by selling the power generated. The private-sector approach would make firm power the most important outcome, and hence issues of agriculture, environment and wildlife would be secondary. So once again, the project priorities – i.e. primary attention to firm power production – of the 1970s planning process emerged. What was also repeated from the planning process of the 1970s was the inability to gain momentum. Even as the MoU was being signed by RUBADA and Odebrecht, Brazil was entering a serious political and economic crisis. In addition Odebrecht was implicated in great schemes of corruption not only in Brazil but also in a number of countries worldwide in order to win contracts.[189] This also led to the withdrawal of Odebrecht from its role as a potential constructor of the Stiegler's Gorge project with support from the Brazilian government.

---

189 BBC News, April 19, 2019, "Odebrecht case: Politicians worldwide suspected in bribery scandal".

References

ACRES (1978): *Tanzania Power Sector Study*. Draft Final Report. Niagara Falls.

Agrar- und Hydrotechnik (1982). Irrigated Agriculture in the Lower Rufiji Valley. Pre-feasibility study, Essen, 1982.

Angwazi and Ndulu (1973). Angwazi, J., and Ndulu, B. Evaluation of Operation Rufiji 1973, *BRALUP Service Paper* No. 73/9, University of Dar es Salaam, 1973.

BBC News, April 17, "Odebrecht case: Politicians worldwide suspected in bribery scandal". https://www.bbc.com/news)/world – latin – america- 41109132.

Cook (1974). Cook, A. Land-Use Recommendations for Rufiji District, *BRALUP Research Report* No. 11 (New Series), University of Dar es Salaam, 1974.

Dye (2017). Dye, B. The Stiegler's Gorge Hydropower Dam Project: A briefing report for WWF. Geneva, 2017.

FAO (1961). *The Rufiji Basin. Tanganyika. Report to the Government of Tanganyika on the preliminary reconnaissance survey of the Rufiji Basin. Volume I, General Report*, FAO, 1961.

Gibbon, Havnevik and Hermele (1993). Gibbon, P., Havnevik, K., and Hermele, K. A *Blighted Harvest: The World Bank and African Agriculture in the 1980s*, James Currey, Oxford and Red Sea Press, Trenton, New Jersey, 1993.

Gillman (1945). Gillman, C. *A Reconnaissance of the Hydrology of the Tanganyikan Territory in its Geographical Settings*, Government Printer, Dar es Salaam, 1945.

Hafslund (1980). *Stiegler's Gorge Power and Flood control Development. Project Planning Report.* Volume I. Oslo, July. Report presented to RUBADA.

Havnevik (1975). Havnevik, K. En vurdering av Norconsults's Stiegler's Gorge Rapport, *DERAP Working Paper* no. A71, Chr. Michelsen Institute, Bergen, 1975.

Havnevik (1978). Havnevik, K. The Stiegler's Gorge Multipurpose project: 1961-1978, *DERAP Working Paper* no. 131, Chr. Michelsen Institute, Bergen, 1978.

Havnevik (1981). Havnevik, K. Stiegler's Gorge Prosjektet: Gir planleggingsmetoden forsvarlig flomsikring?, mimeo, 1981.

Havnevik (1982). Havnevik, K. The Rufiji Delta Mangrove Concession, mimeo, 1982.

Havnevik et al. (1988). Havnevik, K, et al. *Tanzania Country Study*, University of Bergen, 1988.

Havnevik (1993). Havnevik, K. *Tanzania: The limits to development from above*. Chapter 8. Nordic Africa Institute, Uppsala, 1993.

Hoag and Öhman (2008). Hoag, H. J., and Öhman, M-B., Turning Water into Power: Debates over the development of Tanzania Rufiji River Basin, *Technology and Culture*, 49:3 (2008).

Joseph (1979). Joseph, G. An Econometric Approach to Forecasting Demand for Electricity in Tanzania to the year 2000 A.D., *BRALUP Research Report* No. 38, University of Dar es Salaam, 1979.

Marshland (1938). Marshland, H. Mlau-cultivation in the Rufiji Valley, *Tanganyika Notes and Records*, no. 5, Dar es Salaam, 1938.

Nkonoki (1983). Nkonoki, S. R. Cooperation in Energy Development in Eastern Africa, *DERAP Publication* no. 166, Chr. Michelsen Institute, Bergen, 1983.

Norconsult (1972). Stiegler's Gorge Hydropower Utilisation. Power Production, Preliminary report. Norconsult, Oslo, 1972.

Norplan (1983). The Lower Rufiji Valley Integration Study. Norplan, in association with Mr M.D. Segal. Final report, August 1983.

Odebrecht (2013). Stiegler's Gorge Hydropower Project: Presentation of report and proposal, 17 January, 2013.

Öhman (2003). Öhman, M-B. *Swedish energy assistance in a historical perspective,* PhD dissertation, KTH, Stockholm, 2003.

Sandberg (1973). Sandberg, A. Ujamaa and Control of the Environment, paper presented at the East African Universities Social Sciences Conference, Dar es Salaam, 1973.

Sandberg (1974a). Sandberg, A. Socio-economic Survey of Lower Rufiji Flood Plain. Rufiji Delta Agricultural System, *BRALUP Research Paper* No. 34, University of Dar es Salaam, 1974.

Sandberg (1974b). Sandberg, A. The Impact of the SG Dam on Rufiji Flood Plain Agriculture, *BRALUP Service Paper* No. 74/2, University of Dar es Salaam, 1974.

Siderius et al (2018). Siderius, C, et al. Going local: Evaluating and regionalizing a global hydrological model's simulation of riverflows in a medium-sized East African basin, *Journal of Hydrology: Regional Studies 19*, Elsevier, Amsterdam, 2018.

Takouleu (2018). Takouleu, Jean Marie; SENEGAL: AFD and the state are launching projects to protect Langue de Barbarie; Afrik 21; Published on November 8 2018 / Modified on November 8 2018.

Telford (1929). Telford, A. Report on the Development of the Rufiji and Kilombero Valley. Crown Agents for the Colonies, London, 1929.

ToR (1976). Terms of Reference (ToR), the Hafslund study, 1976.

URT (1992). *The Energy Policy of Tanzania.* Ministry of Water, Energy and Minerals, Dar es Salaam, 1992.

USAID (1967). Rufiji Basin: Land and Water Resource Development Plan and Potential, Prepared for USAID by Bureau of Reclamation, US Dept. of the Interior, 1967.

Wangwe (1987). Wangwe, S.M. Impact of IMF/World Bank Philosophy, the Case of Tanzania. In K.J. Havnevik (ed.), *The IMF and the World Bank in Africa.* Scandinavian Institute of African Studies, Uppsala, 1987.

Yoshida (1974). Yoshida, M. *Agricultural Survey of the Lower Rufiji Flood Plain*, Ministry of Water Development and Power, Dar es Salaam, 1974.

Photo: Kevin Harber

Missing in the plan and implementation of the Stiegler's Gorge project is the potential for smallholder irrigation schemes in the lower Rufiji Valley.

/ Kjell Havnevik, p. 109

Coast Region, Tanzania, August 2007.
Men working on an irrigation project.
Photo Scott Wallace, World Bank.

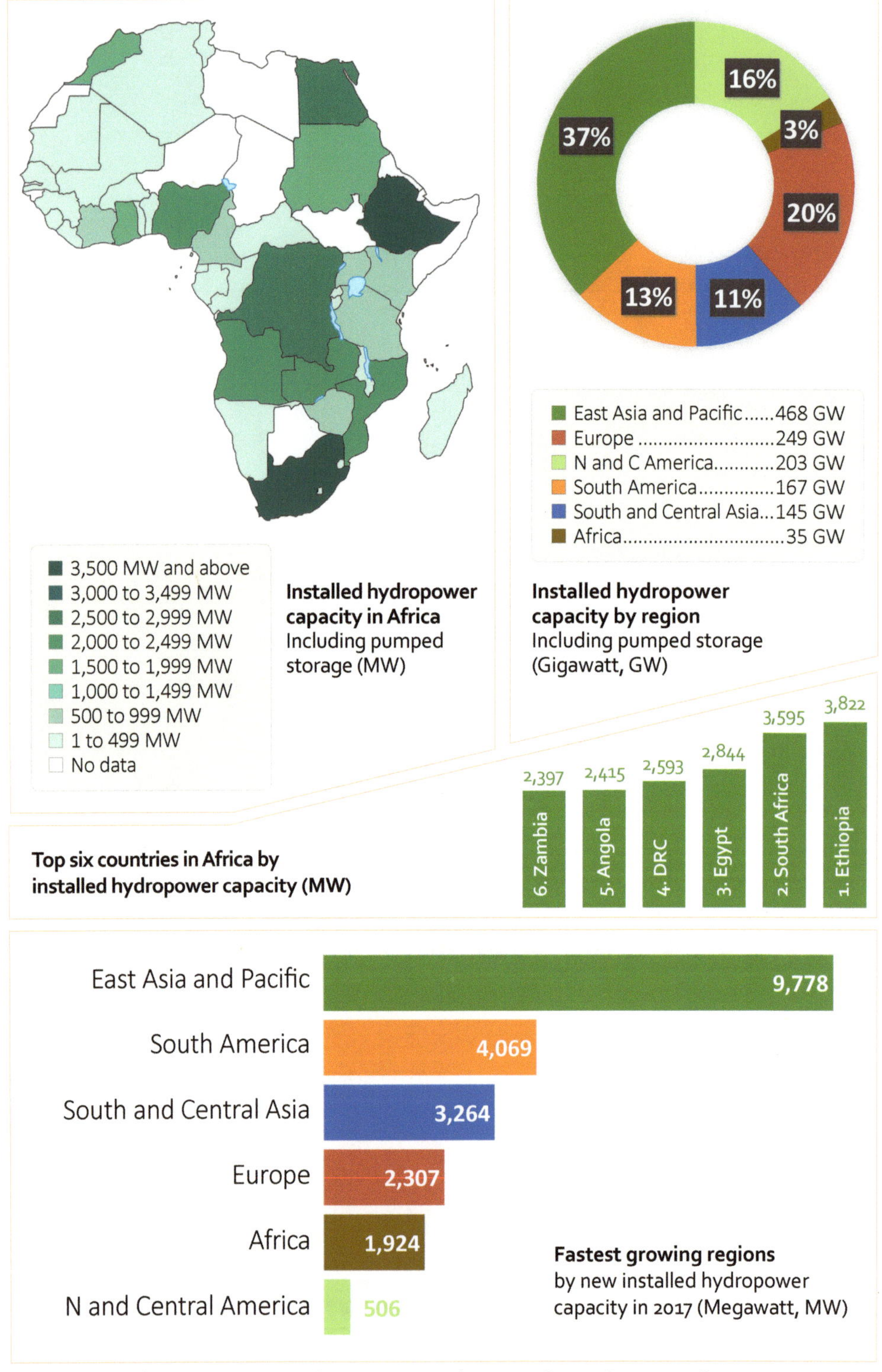

Figure 6.1. Hydropower statistics. Source: IHA, Hydropower Status Report 2018.

CHAPTER 6
The Stiegler's Gorge project in Tanzania: the dam that will be built?

Kjell Havnevik

In August 2017, the Tanzanian Ministry of Energy and Minerals (later divided into two ministries) opened the tendering process for construction of the Stiegler's Gorge project. The specification in the tender followed the Odebrecht plan of 2013 – the hydropower capacity generation should be 2,100 MW and the guaranteed annual firm electricity production was to be 5,992 GWh. In the tender documents, the total reservoir, located inside the Selous Game Reserve, is stated to be 34 billion cubic metres, with a length of 100 km, and the dam height is to be 134 metres. The deadline for the international bidding process was 16 October 2017. In November 2018, the Tanzanian government informed that an Egyptian company had won the contract to implement the Stiegler's Gorge project.

Environmental and wildlife impact

In the meantime, in April 2018, the Ministry of Natural Resources and Tourism and its agency, the Tanzanian Forest Services (TFS), announced a tender for the sale of standing trees comprising nearly 3.5 million cubic metres in Rufiji District.[190] It is estimated that this would mean the felling of 2 million trees within or adjacent to the Selous Game Reserve.

This led to questions being raised by members of parliament about the environmental impact and other aspects of the Stiegler's Gorge project. The response to the government's plan for massive tree felling was that this should wait until a strategic environmental assessment (SEA) had been finalised for the project.[191]

My assessment is that for a large, multi-impact and multipurpose project like Stiegler's Gorge, an SEA is required, rather than the spatially limited environmental impact study (EIA). As discussed in chapter 5, the project will have environmental

---

190 URT (2018).
191 *The Citizen* (Dar es Salaam), 22 May 2018.

and wildlife impacts upstream of the reservoir and its surroundings. Downstream, the project will have a big impact on the Rufiji River flow and – very importantly – the quality of its water. The Rufiji Valley agricultural system is well adapted to flooding: it is based on planting of rice and maize in the long rainy season (*mvuli*) and on planting of cotton, pulses and maize at the time the floodwater withdraws (*mlau*).[192] That flood water currently contains organic silt, which fertilises the land. But the rich silt will be trapped by any future dam.

The change in the water flow and flood profiles will also affect valley river and lake fisheries. There will be several impacts in and near to the Rufiji delta. Increased saltwater intrusion into the delta river channels (caused by lower water flows in the river) is likely to reduce the annual crops of rice in the inner delta agriculture from two to one.[193] The rich prawn fisheries off the Rufiji delta and other fisheries in the Indian Ocean will also be impacted to some extent.[194] In the Rufiji delta, the finely tuned ecological system will feel the effects on the fauna and flora, in particular mangroves. The trapping of silt in the dam is also likely to undermine parts of the delta, and villages close to the coastline are likely to be affected (e.g. Mbwera, Jaja and Pobwe). It is important to note that villagers in the Rufiji River valley and, in particular, the delta areas have diversified their economic activities in order to protect their livelihoods.[195]

The history of the planning of the Stiegler's Gorge project thus reveals the need for comprehensive mapping and analysis of the potential environmental and wildlife impacts, as well as the production and social impacts. In addition, climatic impacts should be investigated. How to reduce or alleviate some of these many impacts through project design and compensation – that represents a great challenge to the implementation and operation of the Stiegler's Gorge project.

Critique from international organisations

In May 2018, the debate about the environmental impacts of Stiegler's Gorge intensified and reached parliament. In this context, the then deputy minister in the Vice President's Office responsible for the Union and the environment, Mr Kangi Lugola, stated that, 'a paper prepared by professor R. Mwalyosi from the University of Dar es Salaam's Institute of Resource Assessment in 2009 would be used as the environmental impact assessment for the Stiegler's Gorge hydropower project'.[196] (Given the large and complicated impacts of the project, it seems clear that a single paper, although of high quality, cannot constitute an SEA of the project.) That same day, however, the Minister of Energy, Dr Medard Kalemani, revealed that 'all environmental procedures will be followed'.[197]

---

192 Havnevik (1993): 97.
193 Hamerlynck, Duvail et al (2011) and Sandberg (1974).
194 Duvail et al (2011).
195 Havnevik (1980) and Havnevik (1993).
196 The Citizen (Dar es Salaam), 22 May 2018.
197 The Citizen (Dar es Salaam), 22 May 2018.

Subsequently, on 28 June 2018, at a meeting of the World Heritage Committee in Bahrain, the permanent secretary in the Tanzanian Ministry of Natural Resources and Tourism, Major General Gaudence Milanzi, reiterated the government's preparedness 'to safely implement the 2,100 MW Stiegler's hydropower plant in the Selous Game Reserve'.[198] Mr Milanzi further stated that UNESCO had agreed to work with Tanzania 'to ensure that the implementation of the project does not impact the environment negatively'. However, on the other side, the Tanzanian government 'reiterated the benefits of the implementation of the project'. *The Citizen* mentioned that the World Wide Fund for Nature (WWF), had released a report on the fringes of the Bahrain meeting, stating that: 'Tanzania will launch a Strategic Environmental Assessment (SEA) of the proposed USD 5 billion dam in the world's [largest] game reserve.'[199]

The WWF is deeply concerned that a proper SEA should be carried out, because a study commissioned by it (and published in July 2017) found that 'the proposed dam threatens both the Selous Game Reserve World Heritage site and the adjacent Rufiji-Mafia-Kilwa Marine Ramsar site'.[200] The International Union for Conservation of Nature (IUCN) is also critical of the Stiegler's Gorge project and has called for it to be abandoned. Unlike the international environmental and animal conservation bodies, the Tanzanian government needs to weigh the potential benefits of the Stiegler's Gorge project against its various adverse effects, before arriving at a decision that is the best one for society, production, employment and the environment in the longer run. This decision must perforce be founded on difficult compromises and trade-offs that go beyond the scope of the international wildlife and environmental conservation organisations.

Anyway, in balancing the benefits and costs to society, it is I believe important for the Tanzanian government to put the Stiegler's Gorge project on a sound environmental footing. This is also necessary in order to mobilise additional support for its implementation both inside the country and abroad. The heads of the relevant Tanzanian ministries (Energy, Natural Resources and Tourism, Agriculture and Industry), as well as state agencies such as the Tanzania Electric Supply Company (TANESCO), the National Environment Management Council (NEMC) and the Rufiji Basin Development Authority (RUBADA) and their advisors, need to gain an overview of existing studies related to the plan for implementation and the impacts of the project. In this framework, Professor Mwalyosi's paper of 2009 and a number of studies in the archives of RUBADA from earlier planning stages of the project are relevant (I have identified 27 important studies, many of which are still relevant but need to be updated).[201] Both domestic and international research that is relevant for an understanding of the project and its potential impacts needs to be identified and scrutinised, including experiences from the implementation and operation of other dam and hydro production projects in various countries (one important source here would be the extensive overview of ex-

---

198 The Guardian (Dar es Salaam), 29 June 2018.
199 The Citizen (Dar es Salaam), 29 June 2018.
200 The Citizen (Dar es Salaam), 29 June 2018. See Dye (2017).
201 Havnevik (1993): Appendix 3: 337–38.

periences contained in the World Commission on Dams report of 2000).[202] With such a broad knowledge basis, it should be possible to ascertain the extent to which an SEA exists for the project, or what is required in the way of new studies and the updating of existing studies to obtain one.

The Tanzanian government has also shown its intention of getting the Stiegler's Gorge project started in other ways – in May 2018 it allocated 700 billion Tanzanian shillings (TZS) in the 2018/19 budget to the project.[203] In 2017, the Tanzanian government approached its Ethiopian counterpart for advice on the project; this later resulted in a visit by Ethiopian experts to Tanzania. Clearly Ethiopia, through massive investment in dams for water supply, smallholder irrigation agriculture and large-scale energy production has accumulated wide experience with similar projects. That country has relied primarily on its own resources, competence and manpower to implement most of those projects, including the huge Renaissance dam and power project, which is nearing completion.[204]

Tanzania will be unable to carry through a project of the size and cost of the Stiegler's Gorge relying just on its own resources. This was acknowledged by the Brazilian company Odebrecht (see Chapter 5), which proposed that the funding of Stiegler's Gorge should be consortium based – the investments being recovered through the sales of the power generated. Such an approach would, however, push the project in a single direction – hydropower production – whereas the project envisages multiple purposes. To avoid such an approach, there is a need to identify and concretise the multiple benefits of the project, as well as the potential adverse impacts.

In this context, another important issue was raised in parliament: what is the relationship between different energy supply sources in Tanzania, now that the country has found and is already supplying natural gas to its citizens? The representative Halima Mdee, 'sought to know how far power generation using natural gas from Mtwara has reached and where the Stiegler's Gorge will start from'.[205] Mrs Mdee also called for answers from the government concerning the failure to transport natural gas through the pipeline that had already been constructed. The deputy minister of energy, Ms Subira Mgalu, responded that the country could not sustain its electricity demand on one source of power. She added that the government's agenda for industrialisation would require the production of 5,000 MW of electricity, and that to attain this the electricity from Stiegler's Gorge would be important, due to its low cost of TZS 36 per unit, compared to TZS 147 per unit for natural gas.[206]

Clearly the economic long-term sustainability of the Stiegler's Gorge project is a critical issue. How much of the demand for electricity can the production (present and future) of natural gas cover and at what cost? How much energy is being produced and

---

202 WCD (2000).
203 The Citizen (Dar es Salaam), 29 June 2018; Michael Harris, 40% of Tanzania's budget proposal allocated for Stiegler's Gorge hydro project, HydroWorld.com, 30 May 2018.
204 A. Cascão, chapter 7 this volume.
205 The Citizen (Dar es Salaam), 11 May 2018.
206 The Citizen (Dar es Salaam), 11 May 2018.

will come on stream in the future, not only in Tanzania, but in the East African region, including Ethiopia? There has to be, as Ms Mgalu stated, a multi-source analysis of current and future energy provision. In addition, it could be stated that this analysis needs to assume a regional perspective.

Regional challenges and missing elements

Hence East African countries, including Ethiopia, need to cooperate to reach the best sustainable solution on energy production for the region. In this, the region must rely on its own balanced analysis of the longer-term benefits and potentials directed towards societal transformation. A long-term transformational strategy for energy demand has also, as Ms Mgalu said, to include plans for industrialisation and technology development. However, in this process past strategic errors have to be addressed and rectified.[207]

On the other hand, industrialisation in Tanzania needs to be linked to regional and/or continental trade cooperation and well-informed plans for the selective protection of industries that need to develop before being exposed to global competition (the infant industry argument). A possible option for the industrialisation of many African countries is to better control their own land and minerals and to process agricultural crops and natural resources further up the commodity value chain. By doing so, 'trading down' can be substituted by a process of 'trading up'.[208]

Missing in the plan and implementation of the Stiegler's Gorge project is the potential for smallholder irrigation schemes in the lower Rufiji Valley. Historically, agricultural development and food production were important drivers for the planning of a dam at Stiegler's Gorge. However, when the post-colonial modernisation paradigm gradually took hold,[209] domestic government and external donor interests converged in the direction of hydropower production. Historical evidence, however, indicates that broad-based economic development cannot occur without the generation of an agricultural surplus (to provide food for the urban population at affordable prices) and export incomes.

Today one of the most important challenges facing Tanzania – and Africa as a whole – is to create the conditions necessary for the generation of an economic surplus in agriculture in a labour-intensive manner. The rapid population increase in Tanzania (and the continent) requires a rapid increase in the provision of jobs and economic activities for large numbers of young people entering working age. In fact, 50 per cent of the estimated 2 billion increase in world population between 2015 and 2050 will come from Africa. This implies that Africa will double its population from its current 1.3 billion to 2.6 billion people in three decades. Labour-intensive smallholder irrigation agriculture is one option to address this challenge. The Ethiopian government has

207 Skarstein & Wangwe (1986).
208 Gibbon & Ponte (2005).
209 Havnevik & Isinika (2010) and Öhman (2003).

acknowledged this by building dams not only for power production, but also for the supply of water to smallholder irrigation schemes.[210] To put Tanzanian (and African) land to large-scale mechanised agriculture, often controlled by international investors and sovereign funds, is a poor choice for a country that seeks to enhance its food security, increase employment for its people and generate income in a sustainable way.[211]

Concluding comments

The construction of dams that can combine the supply of water in a controlled way for agricultural irrigation and power for industrialisation, such as the Stiegler's Gorge project, may – if well planned and executed – make an important contribution to the transformation of society.

The planning and implementation of the Stiegler's Gorge project has placed a strong demand on the government to make well-founded decisions, in particular where major trade-offs are at stake. For such decisions to be conducive to the long-term development of the country, they have to be based on experience and knowledge. The government should therefore welcome and discuss constructive comments and criticism related to the implementation of the Stiegler's Gorge project by parliamentarians, public servants, civil society organisations with concerns that relate to various aspects of the project, and concerned citizens, in particular those that will be directly affected by the project. The process of mobilisation for planning and implementation of the project cannot be based on fear and threats – such as those presented by the then deputy minister in the Vice President's Office, Mr Kangi Lugola (recently promoted to home affairs minister) who, in a Tanzanian parliamentary debate on the project, stated that 'the government will go on with implementation of the project whether you like it or not. Those who are resisting the project will be jailed.'[212]

The Tanzanian government, under its current president, has since 2015 taken steps to improve the governance of state institutions and to fight corruption. Important initiatives have also been taken to better control the country's natural resources and ensure that foreign companies which exploit them to gain high profits (usually taken out of the country) pay reasonable taxes. Sound implementation of the Stiegler's Gorge project will require further improvements in state and public governance at – and between – many levels. But if governance improvements are to be sustainable, they have to be based on experience and knowledge that contribute to the creation of a broad, new social contract for society that rests on improved regulations and planning, a fair distribution of responsibilities and incomes, and effective monitoring and follow-up that can lead society in the direction of social justice, sustained management of natural resources and environmental sustainability.

---

210 Beyene (2018).
211 Abdallah et al (2014); Engström (2018); FAO (2013); Fernandes et al (2012); Havnevik et al (2007); Havnevik (2014); and Neville & Dauvergne (2011).
212 The Citizen (Dar es Salaam), 22 May 2018.

Does the authoritarian path taken by the current Tanzanian government relate to disappointments and frustration regarding the democratic process? The two decades (1995–2015) of multi-party democratic development in Tanzania that led to this government did not contribute much to the social transformation of the country. Its economic structure, which depends primarily on agriculture, minerals and natural resources, remains dominant. The contribution of the manufacturing sector to economic growth has declined, and agricultural strategies have emphasised large-scale investments and interventions in geographical corridors. Despite spells of high growth rates, rural poverty has not declined much. Inequality and corruption have increased in the context of high population growth and migration from rural to urban areas. The celebrated 'afro-optimism' of the last decade, championed by the British journal *The Economist*, is, in my assessment, creating a narrative that paves the way for intensified exploitation of the continent by international investors, rather than that supports its transformation.[213]

In its efforts to bring about social transformation, the Tanzanian government is also facing the interests and influence of multinational corporations, global financial institutions and players, and external wealth and pension funds. To a large extent, these actors decide on the direction and character of foreign direct investments. Their main objective is to increase profits and incomes for their shareholders and for citizens outside Tanzania. Investments in large-scale mechanised agriculture, minerals (including gold and gemstones), forest plantations and natural resources are on the increase and Africa is a major target. The external investors have little or no interest in societal transformation in Africa, since that would obstruct their access to the continent's resources. Development assistance has only a limited role to play in this context.

This chapter sketches out my assessment of the wider global, political and governance context for making decisions about the planning and implementation of Stiegler's Gorge. The Tanzanian government, its institutions and people are facing both external and domestic challenges in the decisions and processes relating to the Stiegler's Gorge project. In November 2018, the Tanzanian government informed that the Egyptian company Arab Contractors had won the bid for building the Stiegler's Gorge hydroelectric dam and project which will be carried out in partnership with Elsewedy Electric Company, another Egyptian firm.[214] By linking up with Egyptian companies and knowledge can the Stiegler's gorge project and Tanzania also benefit from the experience, both positive and negative, from the construction and operation of dams and power stations along the lower Nile?

---

213 Havnevik & Isinika (2010) and Havnevik (2015).
214 Takouleu (2018).

References

Abdallah et al (2014). J. Abdallah, L. Engström, K. Havnevik and L. Salomonsson (2014), Large-scale land acquisitions in Tanzania: A critical analysis of practices and dynamics. In M. Kaag and A. Zoomers (eds), *The Global Land Grab: Beyond the hype*. Zed Books, London.

Beyene (2018). A. Beyene (ed), *Agricultural Transformation in Ethiopia. State Policy and Smallholder Farming*. Zed Books London.

Dye, B (2017). *The Stiegler's Gorge Hydropower Dam Project: A briefing report for WWF*. Geneva.

Engström (2018). L. Engström, *Development Delayed: Exploring the failure of a large-scale agricultural investment in Tanzania to deliver promised outcomes*. Doctoral Thesis No. 2018:40, Faculty of Natural Resources and Agricultural Sciences, Swedish University of Agricultural Sciences, Uppsala.

FAO (2013). *Trends and Impacts of Foreign Investment in Developing Country Agriculture: Evidence from case studies*. FAO, Rome

Fernandes et al (2012). B.M. Fernandes, A. Welch and E.C. Goncalves (2012), *Land Governance in Brazil: A geo-historical review of land governance in Brazil*, International Land Coalition Framing the Debate Series No. 2. International Land Coalition, Rome.

Gibbon (1997). P. Gibbon, Prawns and Piranhas: The political economy of a Tanzanian private sector marketing chain, *Journal of Peasant Studies*, 24/4: 1-86.

Gibbon & Ponte (2005). P. Gibbon and S. Ponte, *Trading Down: Africa, value chains and the global economy*. Temple University Press, Philadelphia, 2005.

Hamerlynck, O., Duvail, S., Vandepitte, L., Kindina, K., Nyingi, D. W., Paul, J-L., Yanda, P. Z., Mwakalinga, A. B., Mgaya, Y. D., and Snoeks, J. (2011): To connect or not to connect? Floods, fisheries and livelihoods in the lower Rufiji floodplain lakes. *Hydrological Sciences Journal*, 56:8, 1436-1451, 2011.

Havnevik (1980). K. Havnevik, Economy and Organization in Rufiji District: The case of crafts and extractive activities, *BRALUP Research Paper* No. 65, University of Dar es Salaam

Havnevik (1993). K. Havnevik, *Tanzania: The limits to development from above*, Nordic Africa Institute, Uppsala, in cooperation with Mkuki na Nyota Publisher, Dar es Salaam.

Havnevik et al (2007). K. Havnevik, D. Bryceson, L.-E. Birgegård, P. Matondi and A. Beyene (eds) (2007), *African Agriculture and the World Bank: Development or impoverishment?* Policy Dialogue No. 1. Nordic Africa Institute, Uppsala, Sweden.

Havnevik (2014). K. Havnevik, *Responsible agricultural investments in developing countries: How to make principles and guidelines effective*, Swedish FAO Committee Publication Series 9. Swedish Ministry of Rural Affairs and the Swedish FAO Committee.

Havnevik (2015). K. Havnevik, The Current Afro-Optimism: A realistic image of Africa? Article in honour of Prof. Tore Linne Eriksen, *FLEKS – Scandinavian Journal of Intercultural Theory and Practice*, 2/2, Oslo.

Havnevik & Isinika (2010). K. Havnevik and A. Isinika (eds), *Tanzania in Transition: From Nyerere to Mkapa*. Mkuki na Nyota Publishers, Dar es Salaam, in association with the Nordic Africa Institute, Uppsala, Sweden and Sokoine University of Agriculture, Morogoro, Tanzania, 2010.

Neville & Dauvergne (2011). K.J. Neville and P. Dauvergne (2011), Biofuels and the politics of mapmaking. *Political Geography* 31.

Öhman (2003). Ohman, M-B. *Swedish energy assistance in a historical perspective,* PhD dissertation, KTH, Stockholm, 2003.

Sandberg (1974). A. Sandberg, Socio-economic Survey of Lower Rufiji Flood Plain. Rufiji Delta Agricultural System, *BRALUP Research Paper* 34, University of Dar es Salaam.

Skarstein & Wangwe (1986). R. Skarstein and S. Wangwe, *Industrial Development in Tanzania: Some critical issues*. Nordic Africa Institute, Uppsala, in cooperation with Tanzania Publishing House, 1986.

Takouleu (2018). Takouleu, Jean Marie; SENEGAL: AFD and the state are launching projects to protect Langue de Barbarie; Afrik 21; Published on November 8 2018 / Modified on November 8 2018.

The Citizen, English language newspaper based in Dar es Salaam.

The Guardian, English language newspaper based in Dar es Salaam.

URT (2018). United Republic of Tanzania (URT), Ministry of Natural Resources and Tourism, 25 April 2018.

WCD (2000). *Dams and Development: A New Framework for Decision-Making*. The Report of the World Commission on Dams (WCD), November 2000. Earthscan Publications, London and Sterling, Virginia, 2000.

Recent hydropolitical history shows Sudan exploring its unique midstream position as a way of negotiating both water and hydraulic infrastructure.

/ Ana Elisa Cascão, p. 130

Tuti Island Beach, Khartoum, Sudan.
April 2018. Photo: Jedrek D, Flickr.

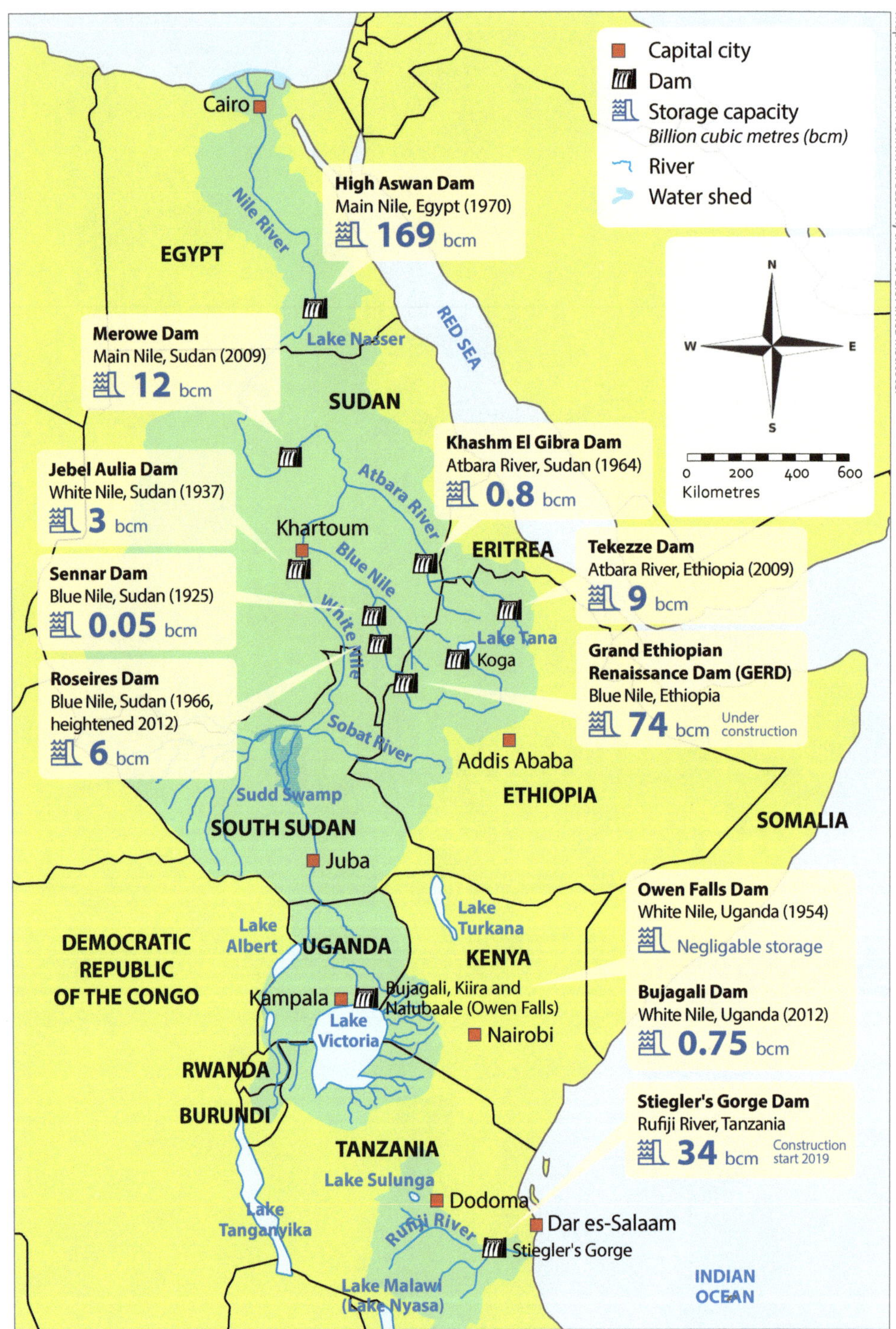

Figure 7.1. The Nile Basin covers approximately 3.25 million square kilometres, about 10 per cent of the area of Africa. Source for data on year of inauguration and approximate storage capacity: Cascão, 2019.

Chapter 7

Storing Nile waters upstream: Hydropolitical implications of dam-building in Sudan and Ethiopia

Ana Elisa Cascão [215]

Variability is the middle name of the Nile River. From several different perspectives, the Nile River Basin is ultimately characterised by complexity and variability. It has a complex geography – the longest river in the world, with several tributaries; it crosses several sovereign countries and administrative borders (see Figure 7.1); it spans different climatic zones with diverse environmental characteristics. On its almost 7,000 kilometres journey, it crosses highlands, deserts, wetlands, cataracts, etc. (see Figure 7.2). Moreover, the tributaries and the various sourcing countries make uneven contributions and have unequal stakes in the system: some countries (e.g. Ethiopia) score high in terms of their contribution to the

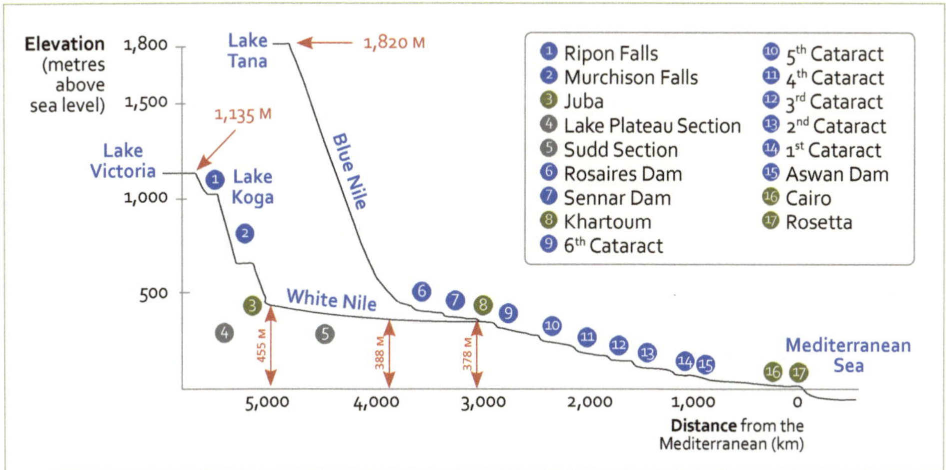

Figure 7.2. The different elevations and lengths of the different tributaries of the Nile Basin. Based on Sutcliffe and Parks, 1999.

---

215 The article was submitted in May 2018. Since then there were many hydropolitical changes which are not captured in the text.

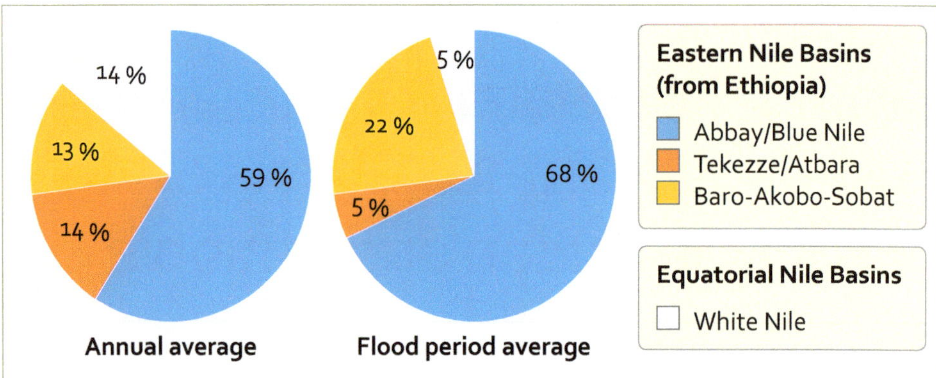

Figure 7.3. Contribution of the Nile flows – by origin. Based on Sutcliffe and Parks, 1999 and Waterbury, 2002.

total water availability in the basin (see Figure 7.3). The Nile Basin also has a complex political economy – millions of people are dependent on its waters, which are used to sustain numerous livelihoods and economic activities. The pressure on the natural resources (water, land, environment) keeps on increasing as the population (and its concomitant demands) grows; meanwhile infrastructure development is failing to keep pace. In a mirror effect, the political and hydropolitical trajectory of the Nile is equally complex and uneven, as analysed later in this chapter.

This section focuses on the impact of uneven hydrology – including intra- and inter-annual water variability – and its implications for the decision-making processes regarding management, allocation and development of Nile water resources. From time immemorial, the Nile has been characterised by irregular flows – which have dictated the socio-economic livelihoods of the people (their spatial distribution, livelihood options, agricultural practices, etc.) from the most upstream catchments to the downstream delta in Egypt, where the Nile flows into the Mediterranean Sea. As visually represented in Figure 7.4, the most striking feature of the Nile Basin is the intra-annual water variability.

The most salient characteristic is the high level of rainfall in the Ethiopian highlands during the months of July to August/September – more precisely in the Blue Nile and Atbara tributaries. These two tributaries – and mainly during those two/three months – are responsible for around 70 per cent of the total annual flow of the Nile (see Figure 7.3). This provides a good indication of the hydrological, hydraulic and hydropolitical importance of the two rivers (in particular the Blue Nile) and the political relevance of their intrinsic variability.

One of the other hydrological characteristics of the Nile River Basin is the inter-annual variability. Several studies and non-academic literature provide a considerable body of evidence of regular periods of drought (as well as other climate extremes, such as floods) throughout the centuries. Contemporary climate science is able to provide detailed analysis for the twentieth and twenty-first centuries. For example, Figure 7.5 below shows the trends for the Blue Nile and Atbara rivers from the 1960s onwards. The infamous severe droughts of the mid-1970s and mid-1980s are clearly visible. So

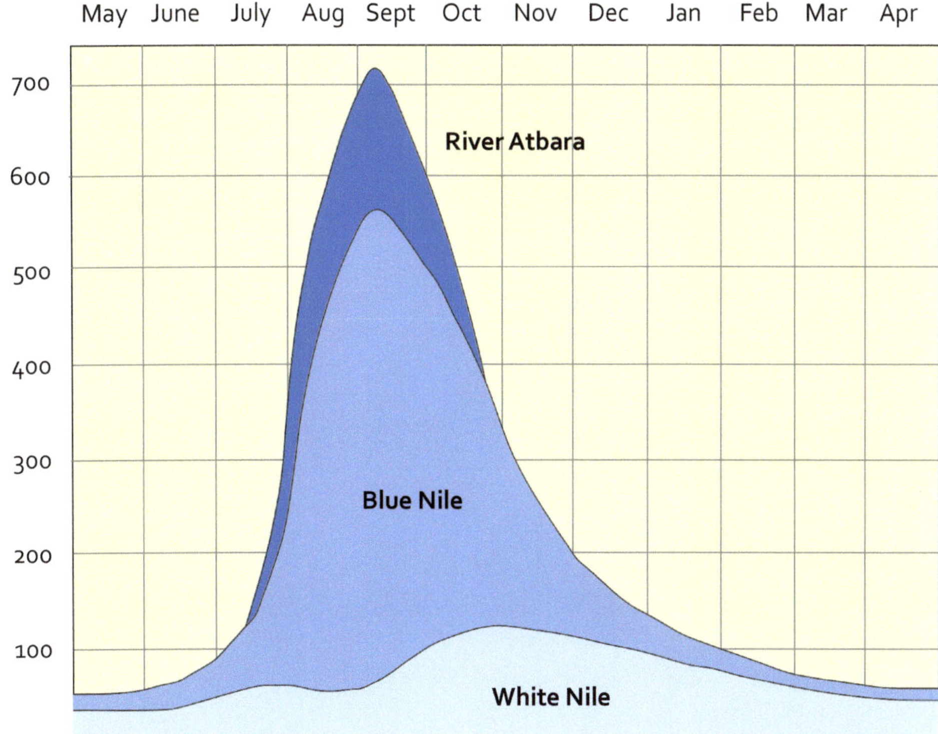

Figure 7.4. Intra-annual variability: distribution of annual flows. Millions of cubic metres per day. Based on Sutcliffe and Parks, 1999.

are the follow-up periods of extremely high flows – for example, toward the mid/end of the 1990s, when it became particularly evident that the Nile Basin region was (and still is) ill-equipped – in terms of storage/infrastructure capacity to deal with significant systemic water surpluses.[216] In this period, even the biggest storage infrastructure in existence in the basin - the High Aswan Dam - was unable to store such a massive volume of water (as discussed later in this chapter).

There are numerous studies on climate-change scenarios for the short-, medium- and long-term future in the Nile Basin. The results of these studies vary, with some predicting more water availability and others increasing shortages; but by and large the studies agree that increasing inter-annual variability in the Nile flows is certain.[217] One of the most recent and high-profile climate studies is forthright: "adequacy of current water storage capacity and plans for additional storage capacity in the basin will need to be re-evaluated given the projected (enhancement of) inter-annual variability in the future flow of the Nile river".[218] Figure 7.6 shows how the existing storage capacities

---

216 Siam and Eltahir, 2017.

217 cf. Conway and Hulme, 1993; Conway, 2005; Golden and Conway, 2008; and Conway, 2017 for a critical and chronological summary of main climate studies – and its main conclusions – as applied to the Nile Basin.

218 Siam and Eltahir, 2017.

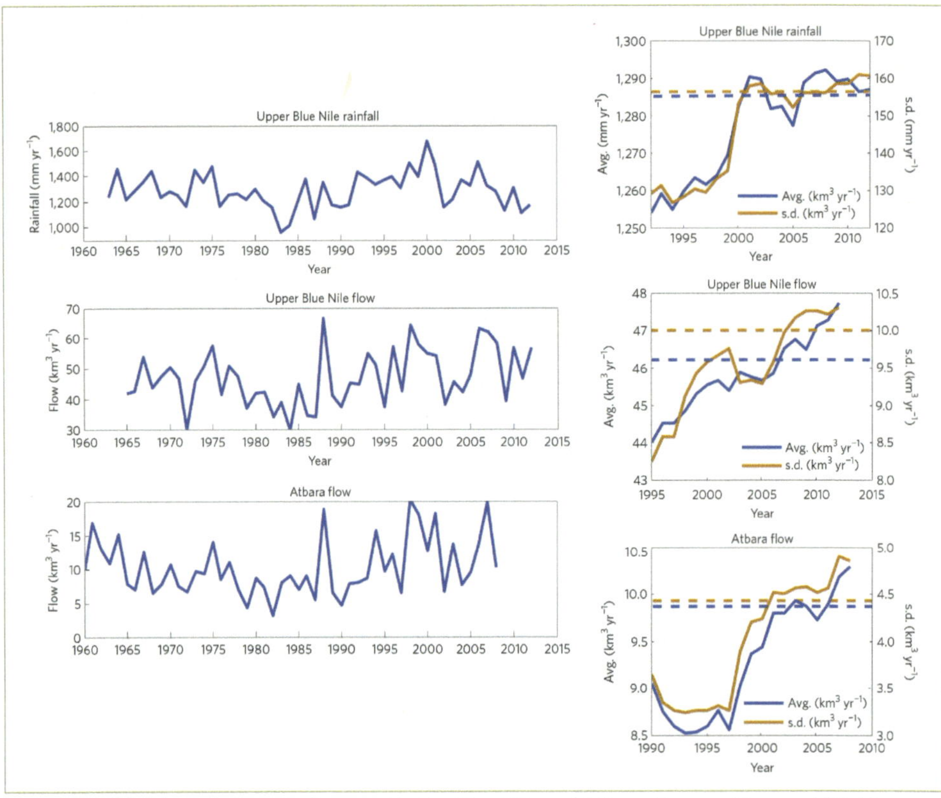

Figure 7.5. Climate variations (1960–2015) in the Blue Nile and Atbara. Source: Siam and Eltahir, 2017.

(including the High Aswan Dam) are actually inadequate to accommodate the expected effects of future climate change.

Storing Nile waters in (and for) Egypt

Egypt – the country whose cultural, socio-economic and political life is most dependent on the Nile, and which is both historically and currently the main user of the Nile's water resources – has long experience of coping with the river's water variability. Over centuries – from the Pharaonic period right up to the Ottomans in the nineteenth century – canals, Nilometers, barrages, pumps, river diversions and (later) storage dams were developed. Technical, social and political engineers were all deployed to study and reduce the risks associated with intra-annual and inter-annual variability: ultimately, this could only be done by increasing control over the mighty but unpredictable river. From the end of the nineteenth century, the British – as the foremost colonial power in the Nile Basin region –investigated the river's hydrology beyond the borders of Egypt and brought the latest and most up-to-date technology to the region. It was during this period that hydraulic infrastructure development gained momentum – the

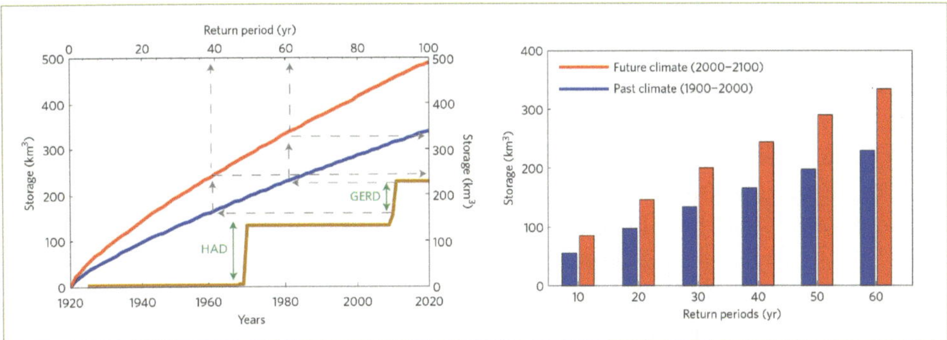

Figure 7.6. Total future storage in the Eastern Nile and required changes in future storage to accommodate climate-change effects. Source: Siam and Eltahir, 2017.

goal of both Egyptian and British engineers was to provide so-called "timely water", i.e. to make water available even in dry and/or drought periods (through storage capacity), in particular for irrigation purposes.

The barrages built in the Nile Valley at the end of the nineteenth century, the Old Aswan Dam in Egypt (1902) and later the Sennar Dam on the Blue Nile in Sudan (1925), the Jebel Aulia Dam on the White Nile in Sudan (1937), the Owen Falls Dam at the outlet of Lake Victoria in Uganda (1954).[219] All these projects were planned and constructed with one thing in mind: to control flooding and promote the storage of water for agricultural development - in Egypt. Storing water during the rainy season (the period of high floods) to be used in drier spells – that is what guided Egypt's hydraulic and hydropolitical strategies in the first half of the twentieth century, in particular with the development of infrastructures within Egypt or in the White Nile sub-basin. As mentioned above, that is not where most of the Nile's waters originate; however, the complex historical relations between Egypt and Ethiopia were always a stumbling block to any talks on possible water storage and savings in the water-rich upstream catchments of the Blue Nile and Atbara rivers. The problem remains to this day, even as a new dam (the first on the Blue Nile in Ethiopia) with a large storage capacity is about to be completed.

The British development approach for the Nile, which was based on several studies of different sections of the basin over long periods of time, evolved towards a "Century Storage Plan", which included developing infrastructure that could offer good storage facilities, with lower evapotranspiration rates than provided by infrastructure built in the desert.[220] The final goal would still be to release the water for utilisation in Egypt – and to a lesser extent in Sudan. However, with the end of the colonial period, the growing nationalist movement in Egypt and President Nasser's ambitious development aspirations, Egypt's hydraulic trajectory took a completely different turn.

Faced with the likely independence of Sudan, in the 1950s the political authorities in Cairo prioritised two interrelated goals: a) construction of a large-scale storage dam

---

219 See Tvedt, 2004.
220 Hurst, 1952.

within Egyptian territory (later named the High Aswan Dam, or HAD), with the capacity to store around 169 billion cubic metres (bcm) annually and potentially capable of doubling the areas of land under irrigation in the Nile Valley and Delta in Egypt; and b) a new legal water agreement with Sudan, the second major user of Nile waters, wherein specific water allocations would be established. This would grant Egypt a major share of the river and simultaneously contain any significant future major agricultural developments in Sudan that could jeopardise Egypt's "right" to the Nile waters. These two elements together represented the end of the British-inspired plans for the Nile Basin,[221] the culmination of Egypt's strategy to gain "full" control over the Nile's waters for its own economic benefit, and the beginning of a hydro-hegemonic context in the region that would, until recently, dominated transboundary political relations between the Nile riparian states.

The bilateral agreement "on the full utilisation of the Nile Waters",[222] signed by Egypt and Sudan in 1959, and the completion of the HAD in 1971 marked the beginning of a new framework of thinking in terms of storage in the Nile Basin. So, besides natural reservoirs such as Lake Victoria or Lake Tana, now there was a new artificial lake downstream – Lake Nasser/Nubia. The HAD has granted Egypt with: 1) the water releases can be fully controlled on a daily basis, to respond to the agricultural plans and demands downstream of the dam; and 2) because of its location in the desert, and the associated high temperatures, the annual evapotranspiration losses are around 10 bcm of water annually – apparently a small price to pay, according to the Egyptian authorities. Besides the HAD, as a result of the 1959 Agreement, other storage reservoirs were also developed in Sudan as a negotiation trade-off: the Khashm El-Girba Dam on the Atbara River (1964) and the Roseires Dam on the Blue Nile (1966). Despite the fact that both are multipurpose dams, their main economic goal has been to support the expansion of irrigated agriculture. However, and not surprisingly, the storage dimensions of these two dams are negligible compared to the HAD (see Figure 7.10). Some 40 years later – in the 2000s – Sudan expanded its storage capacity slightly, first with construction of the Merowe Dam on the main Nile (2009) and then by raising the height of the old Roseires Dam on the Blue Nile by 10 metres (2013). Section 3 discusses Sudan's hydraulic trajectory.

The sanctioned narrative on storage in the Nile Basin has been dominated by the fundamentals described above and could have remained so for many decades to come, had some "emblematic events" not arisen to cast doubt on certain basic assumptions. This chapter looks briefly at two particular developments that have caused the existing hydropolitical setting to be questioned, or even changed. The first took place in the mid-1990s and had natural/climate elements at its root: an abnormal surplus of Nile flows as a result of abundant rainfall levels in the Ethiopia highlands.[223] The second event was more political in nature and gained momentum in April 2011, with the announcement of the Grand Ethiopian Renaissance Dam

---

221 cf. Tvedt, 2004.
222 Agreement, 1959.
223 Waterbury and Whittington, 1998.

(GERD), to be built and financed by the Ethiopian government on its section of the Blue Nile River.[224]

In the mid-1990s, as Figure 7.5 above shows, the total flows of the Nile have increased considerably. But because of the very limited storage capacities in both Ethiopia and Sudan, most of the water kept flowing downstream to Lake Nasser. The consequences were unexpected – the HAD reservoir reached its maximum capacity; this actually put the dam's structure at risk and the decision was taken not to open the dam gates in order to release the vast water surplus, but to divert the surplus away from Lake Nasser to the Toshka Depression in the Western Desert.[225] In 1997, President Hosni Mubarak inaugurated the Toshka (New Valley) Project, a multi-million-dollar project which included agricultural expansion that would create a brand "new civilization" in Egypt.[226]

Twenty years down the line (see Figures 7.7, 7.8 and 7.9), the Toshka project remains shrouded in secrecy and its outcomes difficult to calculate – also confidential remains the information about the amount of Nile waters being used in the schemes or simply stored (and evaporating) in the Toshka Lakes. It lies beyond the scope of this chapter to debate the rationale and consequences of this gigantic (hydro-)political adventure. But the fact that the project was initiated and still persists brings to the forefront a few analytical elements that severely undermine some of the approved narratives: 1) there might be more water in the Nile than suggested by the figures commonly used (a total of 84 bcm/year, as measured at Aswan), but this water remains unaccounted for; 2) the water that is unaccounted for is not necessarily unallocated, because Egypt might be using it in the new and old agricultural schemes; and 3) the out-of-the-basin diversion of the Nile waters as a solution to the water surplus begs a fundamental question: would it not be better for those waters to be stored upstream for the use and benefit of all parties in the future, when abundance might actually give way to scarcity?

Figure 7.7. Toshka Depression before diversion of Nile waters, 1998.

Figure 7.8. New "lakes" in the Toshka Depression after diversion of the Nile waters from Lake Nasser, 2002.

Figure 7.9. New shape of the lakes and new agricultural development in the Toshka region, August 2017.

Source: NASA, 1998.

Source: NASA, 2002.

Source: USGS, 2017.

224 Yihdego et al., 2016, 2017.
225 Conway and Hulme, 1996; Waterbury and Whittington, 1998; Lonergan and Wolf, 2001; Collins, 2006.
226 Baker, 1997.

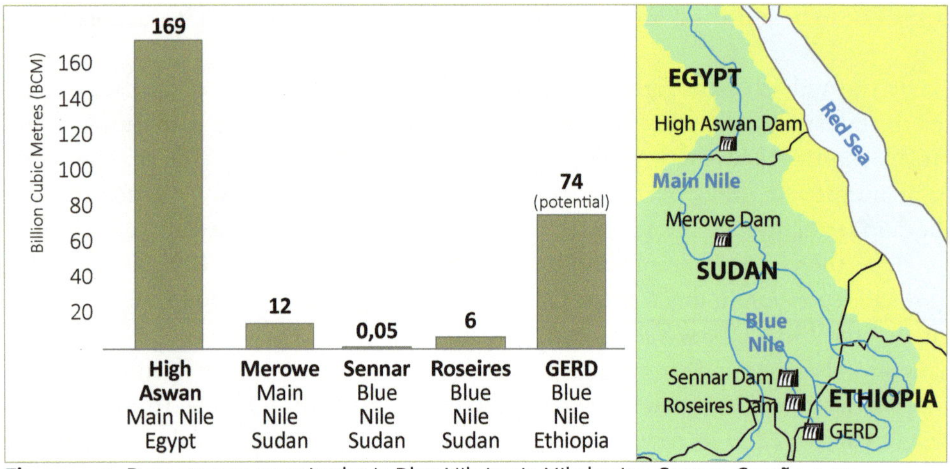

Figure 7.10. Dam storage magnitudes in Blue Nile/main Nile basins. Source: Cascão, 2019.

Storing water upstream: past and current developments

The previous sections already give an indication that development upstream is much smaller than in the downstream catchments. Upstream riparian states have so far not made any substantial use of the Nile water resources in their own countries, and there is very limited irrigation development potential that has been exploited (except in Sudan, as discussed below). This is particularly significant, bearing in mind that irrigation is usually the most water-consumptive use of water resources. Besides, infrastructure development has so far been very limited, in particular when storage is involved. Figure 7.10 shows the storage capacities for all existing (or under construction) hydraulic infrastructure. For purposes of simplification (and because of its larger hydraulic and hydropolitical relevance), this section focuses in particular on the Eastern Nile sub-basin(s). And the question we pose is: what can we observe upstream in terms of storage capacities?

Sudan, the country with the biggest agricultural potential of all the Nile riparian states after Egypt, is already the second main user of the Nile waters and has some storage capacities in place (Sennar, the heightened Roseires, Khashm El-Girba and Merowe dams) that have allowed the country to expand irrigation – but only to a certain extent. In any case, Sudan has a bilateral agreement with Egypt that determines the limit of its water utilisation – i.e. 18.5 bcm of water per year.[227] The potential for Sudan to extend irrigation – even to double current land under cultivation – in its well-known (and supposedly available) fertile lands depends on many things: economic and political stability, investment-friendly factors, access to transport and ports, financial guarantees, etc. But above all, it depends on the availability of "timely water" – just as Egypt needed this in the 1960s to expand its agricultural output. However, as Figure 7.11 below indicates, in order to move forward with the new agricultural expansion, in particular on the banks of the Blue Nile, Sudan would need to augment its storage capacity – which

---

227 Agreement, 1959.

has somehow been exhausted by technical spatial limitations.[228] However, Sudan's limitation is basically restricted to develop storage capacities within its own national borders, but dams upstream in the Ethiopian side of the Blue Nile could provide the much needed storage capacities. And this partially explains the official and public support of the Sudanese government for GERD, almost since its inception in 2011.

	LAND	WATER
Current irrigation (with Old Roseires and Sennar storage)	**1.3 million ha of land** Total area currently under irrigation: • Gezira + Managil: 882,000 ha • Rahad: 148,293 ha • Suki: 29,827 ha • Upstream Sennar: 77,177 ha • Downstream Sennar: 167,200 ha *Total 1,304,497 ha*	**± 3 bcm/year** Total reservoir capacity: • Old Roseires Dam: 3.3 bcm • Sennar: 0.9 bcm *Total 4.2 bcm/year*, but significant storage losses (around 85 per cent in Sennar and 35 per cent in Roseires) due to sedimentation
Full-development scenario	**Additional 0.9 million ha of land** Total area of extended and new schemes: • Extension of Rahad I: 19,740 ha • Rahad II: 210,000 ha • Suki full extension: 2,940 + 3,361 ha • Extension of upstream Sennar: 39,910 ha • Extension of downstream Sennnar: 44,110 + 6,804 ha • New Kenanas II & III: 420,093 ha • New South Dinder: 84,019 + 48,318 ha *Total 879,295 ha*	**Additional 10 bcm/year** Total average annual water demand of extended and new schemes: • Rahad: 2.43 bcm • Suki: 2.2 bcm • Upstream Sennar: 0.75 bcm • Downstream Sennar: 1.5 bcm • Kenana II & III: 2.35 bcm • South Dinder: 0.85 bcm *Total 10,08 bcm/year*

Figure 7.11. Summary of land and water requirements of the Blue Nile irrigation schemes in Sudan (Source: Cascão and Nicol, 2016a).

If we go back to basics: an awareness of Sudan's great potential to become a major user of Nile waters on account of its large irrigation potential has always guided Egypt's hydropolitical stance on Sudan. The 1959 agreement allocations – 55.5 bcm for Egypt and 18.5 bcm for Sudan (plus 10 bcm for evapotranspiration, which then makes the total 84 bcm) – clearly set the limits.[229] The fact is that up until recently, Sudan did not even use the 18.5 bcm/year total defined as its "historical right", and nor did it store its unused waters (because of lack of storage capacity). But the situation has been changing rapidly – and in three different ways.

---

228 See Cascão and Nicol, 2016a for detailed analysis of the trajectory of investments in hydraulic and agriculture infrastructure over the last decade

229 Agreement, 1959.

Figure 7.12. Late Project Manager Eng. Semegnew Bekele at the GERD'S saddle dam, July 2016.

First, Sudan is increasingly open to all kinds of foreign and national investors in the field of commercial agriculture – namely sugar and fodder crops – and as such there are increasing water withdrawals.[230] This trend is expected to increase, as more investors are expected to arrive after the lifting of economic sanctions and the US embargo at the end of 2017. Second, the Merowe Dam located on the main Nile is a hydropower (not storage) dam, but it has increased Sudan's utilisation because of its high levels of evapotranspiration; thus, since the completion of this dam, part of the unused "surplus" has not been flowing downstream to Lake Nasser, as in the past. Third, with the GERD coming into existence, among many other advantages (flood control, sedimentation control, access to cheap electricity, etc.), Sudan sees it as a unique opportunity that did not exist before: in principle, it will be able to store its current unused water from the 18.5 bcm/year in the GERD reservoir and use it progressively in the planned expansion of its new irrigation schemes (see the table above). This will eventually lead to a situation whereby Sudan can actually make full use of its "historical right", as defined in the 1959 Agreement, depriving Egypt of the surplus – or "water loan", as it is usually called by Sudanese authors.[231]

Despite the seriousness of this emerging new hydropolitical reality, if Sudan respects the 1959 agreement allocations, it will be difficult for Egypt to challenge these developments. However, if (as some authors argue) Sudan's agricultural expansion leads to utilisation of 30–32 bcm per year[232] – and if the Sudanese government reveals

---

230 Conniff et al., 2012; McCartney et al., 2012; Sandström et al., 2016.
231 cf. El-Zain 2007.
232 Taha, 2010; Arjoon et al., 2014.

an intention to increase its current water quota – then the political and legal implications would be immense. However, since this is currently not a likely scenario, it falls outside the scope of this article.

In brief, recent hydropolitical history shows Sudan exploring its unique midstream position as a way of negotiating both water and hydraulic infrastructure, in order to expand its agricultural potential. As a background to these new developments, there is renewed hope that this second attempt to become a "breadbasket" will be more successful than the first one in the 1980s, and that Sudan can go beyond the current 18 million hectares currently being cultivated (of which around 2 million hectares are irrigated) and explore part of its huge potential – estimated to be around 105 million hectares. Further developments depend on appropriate hydraulic infrastructure – and, above all, storage capacity. However, Sudan's agricultural potential is dependent on storage upstream of its national borders, and that is why it has always been supportive of a cascade of dams in the Blue Nile, which should regularise the timing of flows, increase water availability during dry months and allow Sudan to irrigate during these months, thus strengthening its agricultural production and output. As a Sudanese official has stated "the GERD is for Sudan what the High Aswan Dam has been for Egypt in the 1970s: an amazing opportunity to increase almost twofold land under irrigation".[233]

This brings us to the second "emblematic event" mentioned above: the ongoing construction of the GERD in the Blue Nile, the technical and political processes surrounding it since the beginning of 2011, and all the implications of this symbolic dam in the overall hydropolitical process and relations in the Nile Basin.[234] The GERD – due to its dimensions and characteristics, is expected to change the way in which the Nile River is both managed and perceived. The GERD, with its 74 bcm of total storage capacity (despite being a hydropower dam), might come not just to regulate the river, its variability and its flows regime, but also to induce many other changes. Several authors call attention to the fact that the operations of the downstream dams in Sudan and Egypt will have to be adapted to the new reality – a major infrastructure that might affect the water availability/flows, in particular during the filling of the GERD.[235]

Ultimately, calculation of the impact and benefits (be technical or economic) of GERD downstream depends a lot on the knowledge to be shared between countries concerning the current figures for use and sectoral allocation of the Nile water resources. This is crucial to define a baseline and a methodology for how to calculate the risks and impacts (as well as the benefits) for all three countries, and later to establish the best approaches to coordination of the different existing and future infrastructures.[236] Because of the longstanding politicisation of figures regarding actual water uti-

---

233 Sudanese official, 2013 in Cascão and Nicol, 2016a.
234 Yihdego et al., 2016, 2017.
235 MIT, 2014; Wheeler et al., 2016; Zhang et al., 2016.
236 Whittington et al., 2014; Arjoon et al., 2014; MIT, 2014; Wheeler et al., 2016; Wheeler, 2017; Boehlert et al., 2017.

lisation,[237] any study or discussion is bound to open up a long and detailed debate about how much water is actually available and will reveal possible overallocation of water resources in certain sectors and/or countries; on the other hand, these studies are also bound to show how more efficient and optimised the system can actually become.

Consequently, discussion about moving storage upstream is coming to the fore because of its centrality in promoting more sustainable, long-term and mutually beneficial water storage to tackle problems related to intra- and inter-annual variability, as well as possible extreme climate scenarios. Although a lot of scientific literature has dealt with the topic, the fact is that political discourse and action have a long way to go before they use hydro-economic studies to guide the decision-making process. Instead, since 2011 we have witnessed the Eastern Nile countries engaged in a technical-cum-political process that has brought several changes: trilateral technical talks, trilateral legal agreements and regular meetings on diverse politico-diplomatic topics.[238] But the fact is that the discussion on the economic benefits and trade-offs associated with the GERD (or any new infrastructure upstream, for that matter) do not appear as a priority on the political agenda at the regional level.

A close analysis of the GERD – both as an infrastructure and as a process – from different perspectives,[239] shed light on a number of significant changes and/or challenges that are bound to guide current and future perceptions, discussions and decisions in the Nile Basin:

- The symbolic power of the GERD: the first dam ever on the Ethiopian section of the Blue Nile, the river that contributes the most to the total Nile flows, is bound to have social, cultural and political impacts for the Eastern Nile riparian states.

- The Nile is gaining a new uniqueness, by virtue of having two large-scale storage sites in the same river system (see Figure 7.10).

- The GERD, despite being a hydropower dam, has opened a revealing discussion about multipurpose projects, multi-sectoral allocations of water, losses in the system, potential to decrease water risks, opportunities for water savings and increased yields.

- It has also generated very fundamental discussions on key knowledge issues, such as: figures (total amounts and averages), baselines (historical, current and actual uses), scenarios (future uses – who and how?) and finally options (how and where can water be utilised in the most efficient manner?).

- The economic discussion regarding benefits and impacts is now more focused on macro- or regional levels, namely when issues such as trade and markets are at stake.

- A clear message from all sides that genuine trilateral coordination and cooperation (going well beyond legal agreements) must be in place to guide any discussions

---

237 Cascão, 2008, 2009, 2013.
238 Cascão and Nicol, 2016a, 2016b, 2017; Tawfik, 2015, 2016, 2017.
239 See several contributions in the edited work of Yihdego, Rieu-Clarke and Cascão, 2016; 2017.

on the filling and long-term operations of the GERD, in order to understand the strategies/options/scenarios available.

- Related to the previous point, the three countries have gone a long way in the process, and several achievements can be listed: the establishment of a functional trilateral joint committee (the GERD Trilateral National Committee - TNC) in 2011; regular meetings at all levels and involving all kinds of technical and political stakeholders; collective decisions on studies, terms of reference, teams, etc., as well as agreement on how to run independent studies throughout the processes; and the first trilateral agreement – the Declaration of Principles (DoP) between the three parties, signed in March 2015.[240]

- However, the GERD process – which took place outside the framework of the multilateral Nile Basin Initiative (namely outside the Eastern Nile Technical Regional Office (ENTRO)/Nile Basin Initiative (NBI) and also the Cooperative Framework Agreement (CFA)[241] – might also be understood as a sub-optimal approach to transboundary water management and development in the Eastern Nile Basin. Ideally this dam (and others) would have been studied, developed and implemented under the auspices of ENTRO/NBI.[242] Likely, this would mean that the project would embrace a priori identification of the purposes, benefits, scale, timeline, etc. in a collective and holistic fashion, instead of on a project-by-project, piecemeal and ad hoc basis. The opportunity was there, but it was missed due to political considerations.

- As has been written elsewhere,[243] the GERD process (both its constructive and its negative sides) should be used to shape future cooperation: this might have to include a reflection? process to consider the advantages and disadvantages of having parallel processes of cooperation on the same river(s) and the extent to which several processes can coexist. Ultimately, it can be questioned if several parallel processes do not pose the risk of undermining the objectives of joint planning and management of common water resources. A critical thinking process will need to question the enormous transaction costs associated with dealing with such a large and complex basin in a project-by-project basis.

- In brief, the GERD process should ultimately provide a strategic opportunity for Nile riparian countries to reflect on the pressing need for a new sustainable and effective transboundary water "regime" in the Nile Basin.

---

240 Agreement, 2015; see also Salman, 2016.
241 Agreement, 2010.
242 cf. Blackmore and Whittington, 2008; NBI, 2014.
243 Cascão and Nicol, 2016b; 2017.

Hydropolitical implications of moving storage upstream – focus on the future

Historically speaking, the Nile River has always been characterised by variability – dealing and coping with natural hydrological and climatic changes is intimately connected with the development of the water resources and any hydraulic infrastructure since at least the Pharaonic period. Over the past half century, the complexity associated with natural variability has been augmented by an immense amount of change at the social, economic, political and geopolitical levels in all the Nile countries and in the region as a whole. Decisions about how to utilise the Nile waters have always guided hydropolitical relations between the Nile riparian states, and implicitly there has always been the issue of storage as a way to minimise the risks associated with floods and droughts, and at the same time to allow the control of flows in order to increase agricultural output. Due to the large degrees of intra- and inter-annual variability in the basin, the management and allocation of Nile water resources imply the development of storage capacities. This chapter has analysed the past and current situations; but what about the future?

Egypt and Sudan have almost exhausted their storage capacities, and even the existing capacities are being questioned on account of their locations and the huge regular water loss due to evapotranspiration in the reservoirs of dams such as the High Aswan or Merowe. Ethiopia will finalise the GERD in the medium-term future, a dam with the second-biggest storage capacity in the basin (equivalent to around 40 per cent of the total storage capacity of the High Aswan Dam), although its main function is not storage, but hydropower. One question remains: is Ethiopia – alone and/or in cooperation with its downstream neighbours – planning to build more dams on the Blue Nile and the other Nile tributaries? As for the future, are the Nile riparian countries keen to collaborate a priori (instead of ad hoc) in an agreed solution on how to promote and maintain coordination between the different existing and future infrastructures – eventually contributing to minimise net losses and increase collective safety nets in case of extreme climate trajectories?

The latest developments in the first half of 2018 (this chapter was written in May 2018) show that Ethiopia, Egypt and Sudan are keen to reach agreement at the highest level – including heads of state and heads of security agencies, along with diplomats and technical experts – and to find a negotiated solution to several critical issues related to infrastructure development. In the short term, the countries have agreed to establish a specialised trilateral working group (National Independent Scientific Research Study Group – NISRSG) to study the different possible scenarios for filling the GERD. If mutual trust, strategic vision beyond water and economic rationale can guide the process, and if the time limitations are overcome, we might soon have an agreement on how to fill the GERD in a way that will minimise possible impact on downstream riparian countries. In the medium term, the Eastern Nile countries have decided to establish a Tripartite Infrastructure Fund (TIF) to provide support for joint infrastructure and development proposals in the three countries. It sounds promising, but still vague, since it does not specify what kind of projects and for what purposes. At the same time, it seems to overlap with the work being done by the NBI and ENTRO, which have spent the past two decades identifying potential joint investment projects.[244]

In any case, it is welcome that investment and economic perspectives are clearly being included in this kind of agreement. However, it is in the long-term perspective that the development (or not) of storage capacities in the Nile Basin should be discussed. What are the needs and the demands, of which country and of which sectors? What are the trade-offs one needs to take account of if a water–food–energy–climate approach is to be adopted? What arrangements should be made (and what institution should be responsible) for conducting studies, developing scenarios and designing possible technical, economic and political tools that should be adopted to make an investment-oriented approach a working reality on the ground with actual tangible benefits? The consensus may be that the best way of doing this is through a regional permanent and trusted institution that can be given additional powers to guide, coordinate and/ or advise decision makers in their policy options and strategic choices regarding the future development of hydraulic infrastructure, in particular where storage is involved.

---

244 NBI, 2014, 2016.

References

Agreement. (1959, November 8). Agreement between the Republic of the Sudan and the United Arab Republic for the full utilization of the Nile waters. Signed at Cairo, Egypt.

Agreement. (2010, May 14). Agreement on the Nile River Basin Cooperative Framework. Signed at Entebbe, Uganda.

Agreement. (2015, March 24). Agreement on Declaration of Principles between the Arab Republic of Egypt, the Federal Democratic Republic of Ethiopia and the Republic of the Sudan on the Grand Ethiopian Renaissance Dam project. Signed at Khartoum, Sudan.

Arjoon, D., Mohamed, Y., Goor, Q. and Tilmant, A. (2014) Hydro-economic risk assessment in the Eastern Nile River Basin. In Water Resources and Economics, 8: 16-31.

Baker, M.M. (1997). "Mubarak: Toshka Project Opens Way Towards New Civilization In Egypt". In The Executive Intelligence Review, December 1997.

Blackmore, D., & Whittington, D. (2008). Opportunities for cooperative water resources development on the Eastern Nile: Risks and rewards. An independent report of the scoping study team to the Eastern Nile Council of Ministers. Washington, DC: World Bank.

Boehlert, B.; Strzepek, K.M.; and Robinson, S. (2017). "Analysing the economy-wide impacts on Egypt of alternative GERD filling policies", In Yihdego, Z., Rieu-Clark, A., and Cascão, A.E. (eds.). The Grand Ethiopian Renaissance Dam and the Nile Basin: Implications for transboundary water cooperation. London: Routledge.

Cascão, A. E. (2008). "Ethiopia – Challenges to Egyptian hegemony in the Nile Basin". In Water Policy, 10 (S2), 13–28.

Cascão, A. E. (2009). "Changing power relations in the Nile River Basin: Unilateralism vs. cooperation?". In Water Alternatives, 2 (2): 245–268.

Cascão, A. E. (2012). "Nile Water Governance". In S. B. Awulachew, V. Smakhtin, D. Molden, & D. Peden (Eds.), The Nile River Basin – Water, agriculture, governance and livelihoods. Abingdon: Routledge, 229-252.

Cascão, A.E. and Nicol, A. (2016a). "Sudan, 'kingmaker' in a new Nile hydropolitics: negotiating water and hydraulic infrastructure to expand large-scale irrigation". In E. Sandström, A. Jägerskog, and T. Oestigaard (eds.), Land and Hydropolitics in the Nile River Basin: Challenges and New Investments. London: Routledge: 89-116.

Cascão, A.E. and Nicol, A. (2016b). "Grand Ethiopian Renaissance Dam (GERD): New Norms of Cooperation in the Nile Basin?". In Water International, Special Issue, 41(4): 550-573.

Cascão, A.E. (2019). "To change, or not to change? The transboundary water question in the Nile Basin". In Olsson, G.A. and Gooch, P. (eds.) Natural Resource Conflicts and Sustainable Development, London: Routledge.

Collins, R.O. (2006). "Negotiations and exploitation of the Nile waters at the end of the Millennium". In Water International, 31(1): 116-126.

Conniff, K., Molden, D., Peden, D. and Awulachew, S. B. (2012). "Nile Water and Agriculture: Past, Present and Future." In Awulachew, S. B., Smakhtin, V., Molden, D. and Peden, D. (eds). The Nile River Basin: Water, Agriculture, Governance and Livelihoods. New York: Routledge: 5–29.

Conway, D. & Hulme, M. (1993). Recent fluctuations in precipitation and runoff over the Nile sub-basins and their impact on Main Nile discharge. Climatic Change 25: 127–151.

Conway, D. and Hulme, M. (1996).."The impacts of climate variability and climate change in the Nile Basin on future water resources in Egypt". In International Journal of Water Resources Development, 12(3): 277-296.

Conway, D. (2005). From headwater tributaries to international river: observing and adapting to climate variability and change in the Nile basin. Glob. Environ. Change 15: 99–114.

Conway, D. (2017). Water resources: future Nile river flows. Nature Climate Change, 7(5): 319-320.

El-Zain, M. (2007). Environmental Scarcity, Hydropolitics, and the Nile. Maastricht, Netherlands: Shaker Publishing.

Goulden M. and Conway D. (2008). Cooperation and adaptation to climate change in the River Nile Basin. In Nile Basin Discourse Forum 2008. Khartoum: Nile Basin Initiative, 580-598.

MoFED (Ministry of Finance and Development, Ethiopia) (2010). Growth and Transformation Plan (GTP) 2010/2011–2014/2015. Addis Ababa: MoFED.

Hurst, H. E. (1952). The Nile: a general account of the river and the utilization of its waters. Constable: London.

Lonergan, S. and Wolf, A.T. (2001).."Moving Water to Move People The Toshka Project in Egypt A Water Forum Contribution". In Water International, 26 (4): 589-596.

MIT (2014). The Grand Ethiopian Renaissance Dam: An opportunity for collaboration and shared benefits of the Eastern Nile Basin. An Amicus brief to the Riparian Nations of Ethiopia, Sudan and Egypt from the International, Non-partisan Eastern Nile Working Group. Convened at the Massachusetts Institute of Technology on 13–14 November 2014 by the MIT Abdul Latif Jameel World Water and Food Security Lab. Cambridge, MA: MIT.

McCartney, M., Alemayehu, T., Easton, Z., & Awulachew, S. (2012). "Simulating current and future water resources development in the Blue Nile river basin". In S. B. Awulachew, V. Smakhtin, D. Molden, & D. Peden (Eds.), The Nile River Basin – Water, agriculture, governance and livelihoods. Abingdon: Routledge: 269–291.

NASA (1998). NASA Earth Observatory. Available in https://wp.usit.ie/2016/11/30/google-earths-updated-timelapses-will-amaze-inspire-and-scare-you/toshka-1998/

NASA (2002). NASA Earth Observatory. Available in https://visibleearth.nasa.gov/view.php?id=57923

Nile Basin Initiative (2014). Nile cooperation: Opportunities and challenges (Flagship Paper). Entebbe: NBI

Nile Basin Initiative (2016). Nile Basin Water Resources Atlas. Entebbe: NBI

Salman, M. A. S. (2016). "The Grand Ethiopian Renaissance Dam: The road to the Declaration of Principles and the Khartoum document". In Water International. 41(4): 1-16.

E. Sandström, A. Jägerskog, and T. Oestigaard (eds.) (2016). Land and Hydropolitics in the Nile River Basin: Challenges and New Investments. London: Routledge

Siam, S.S. and Eltahir, E.A.B. (2017). "Climate change enhances interannual variability of the Nile river flow.". In Nature Climate Change, 7: 350-354.

Sutcliffe, J. V. and Parks, Y. (1999) The hydrology of the Nile. IAHS Publication 5. Wallingford: IAHS Press.

Taha, F., (2010) The history of the Nile waters in the Sudan. In Tvedt, T. The River Nile in the Post- Colonial Age: Conflict and Cooperation among the Nile Basin Countries. IB Tauris, London, 179–216.

Tawfik, R. (2015). Revisiting hydro-hegemony from a benefit- sharing perspective: the case of the Grand Ethiopian Renaissance Dam. Deutsches Institut für Entwicklungspolitik Discussion paper, issue 5, 2015.

Tawfik, R. (2016). "The Grand Ethiopian Renaissance Dam: a benefit-sharing project in the Eastern Nile?". In Water International, Special Issue, 41(4), 574-592.

Tawfik, R. and Dombrowsky, I. (2017). "GERD and hydropolitics in the Eastern Nile: from water to benefit sharing?", In Yihdego, Z., Rieu-Clark, A., and Cascão, A.E. (eds.). The Grand Ethiopian Renaissance Dam and the Nile Basin: Implications for transboundary water cooperation. London: Routledge.

Tvedt, T. (2004). The River Nile in the age of the British – Political ecology and the quest for economic power. London: IB Tauris.

USGS (United States Geological Service) (2017). Toshka Project, Egypt in Earthshots: Satellite Images of Environmental Change. Available in https://earthshots.usgs.gov/earthshots/node/62#ad-image-0-0

Waterbury, J. (2002). The Nile Basin national determinants of collective action. New Haven, CT: Yale University Press.

Waterbury, J. and Whittington, D. (1998). "Playing Chicken on the Nile? The Implications of Microdam Development in the Ethiopian Highlands and Egypt's New Valley Project". In Natural Resources Forum, 22(3): 155-163.

Wheeler, K. et al. (2016) "Cooperative filling approaches for the Grand Ethiopian Renaissance Dam". In Water International, Special Issue, 41(4): 611-634.

Wheeler, K. ((2017). "Managing risks while filling the Grand Ethiopian Renaissance Dam", In Yihdego, Z., Rieu-Clark, A., and Cascão, A.E. (eds.). The Grand Ethiopian Renaissance Dam and the Nile Basin: Implications for transboundary water cooperation. London: Routledge.

Whittington, D.; J. Waterbury; M. Jeuland (2014). "The Grand Renaissance Dam and Prospects for Cooperation on the Nile.". In Water Policy, 16: 595-608.

Yihdego, Z., Rieu-Clark, A., and Cascão, A.E. (eds.) (2016). "The Grand Ethiopian Renaissance Dam: Legal, Political and Scientific Challenges. Water International, Special Issue, 41 (4), 503-651.

Yihdego, Z., Rieu-Clark, A., and Cascão, A.E. (eds.) (2017). The Grand Ethiopian Renaissance Dam and the Nile Basin: Implications for transboundary water cooperation. London: Routledge.

Zhang, Y., Erkyihum, S. T., and Block, P. (2016). "Filling the GERD: Evaluating hydroclimatic variability and impoundment strategies for Blue Nile riparian countries". In Water International, 41(4): 593–610.

Blue Nile Falls, Ethiopia. Photo: Alex Keshavjee.

Index

Current African Issues (CAI)

Current African Issues (CAI) is a book series published by the Nordic Africa Institute since 1981. As the title implies, it raises and analyses current and topical issues concerning Africa. All CAI books are academic works by researchers in the social and multidisciplinary sciences. Listed below are some previous titles in the CAI series:

65 *Land Tenure Dynamics in East Africa : The Changing Practices and Rights to Land;* Opira OTTO, Aida ISINIKA and Herman MUSAHARA (eds); 2019

64 *The Nuer Pastoralists : Between Large Scale Agriculture and Villagization;* Wondwosen Michago SEIDE; 2017

63 *Agricultural water institutions in East Africa;* Atakilte BEYENE (ed); 2015

62 *Dammed divinities : the water powers at Bujagali Falls, Uganda;* Terje OESTIGAARD; 2015

61 *African conflicts, development and regional organisations in the post-Cold War international system;* Victor A. O. ADETULA; 2015

60 *The role of food banks in food security in Uganda : the case of the Hunger Project food bank, Mbale epicentre;* Joseph WATULEKE; 2015

59 *Resettled for development : the case of New Halfa agricultural scheme, Sudan;* Marianna WALLIN; 2014

58 *Youth and the labour market in Liberia : on history, state structures and spheres of informalities;* Emy LINDBERG; 2014

57 *Current status of agriculture and future challenges in Sudan;* Farida MAHGOUB; 2014

56 *Election-related violence : the case of Ghana;* Clementina AMANKWAAH; 2013

55 *Academics on the move : mobility and institutional change in the Swedish development support to research capacity building in Mozambique;* Måns FELLESSON and Paula MÄHLCK; 2013

54 *The oil industry in Uganda : a blessing in disguise or an all too familiar curse?;* Pamela K. MBABAZI; 2013

53 *Sweden-Norway at the Berlin conference 1884-85 : history, national identity-making and Sweden's relations with Africa;* David NILSSON; 2013

52 *Musical violence : gangsta rap and politics in Sierra Leone;* Boima TUCKER; 2013

51 *Favouring a demonised plant : Khat and Ethiopian smallholder enterprise;* Gessesse DESSIE; 2013

50 *From global land grabbing for biofuels to acquisitions of African water for commercial agriculture;* David Ross OLANYA; 2012

49 *Water scarcity and food security along the Nile : politics, population increase and climate change;* Terje OESTIGAARD; 2012

48 *Transnational activism networks and gendered gatekeeping : negotiating gender in an African association of informal workers;* Ilda LINDELL; 2011

47 *Natural resource governance and EITI implementation in Nigeria;* Musa ABUTUDU and Dauda GARUBA; 2011

46 *African migration, global inequalities, and human rights : connecting the dots;* William MINTER; 2011

45 *The agrarian question in Tanzania? : a state of the art paper;* Razack B. LOKINA, Sam MAGHIMBI and Mathew A. SENGA; 2011

44 *Understanding poverty in Africa? : A navigation through disputed concepts, data and terrains;* Mats HÅRSMAR; 2010.

43 *China, India, Russia and the United States : The Scramble for African Oil and the Militarization of the Continent;* Daniel VOLMAN; 2009.

42 *Persuasive prevention : Towards a Principle for Implementing Article 4(h) and R2P by the African Union;* Dan KUWALI; 2009.

You can find these, and earlier titles in the CAI series, in our digital archive Diva, www.diva-portal.org, where they are also available as open access resources for any user to read or download at no cost.